EXPLORING THE UNSAID

EXPLORING THE UNSAID
Creativity, Risks and Dilemmas in Working Cross-Culturally

Edited by
Barry Mason & Alice Sawyerr

Foreword by
Nancy Boyd-Franklin

Systemic Thinking and Practice Series

Series Editors
David Campbell & Ros Draper

LONDON AND NEW YORK

First published in 2002 by
Karnac Books Ltd.

Published 2018 by Routledge
2 Park Square, Milton Park, Abingdon, Oxon OX14 4RN
711 Third Avenue, New York, NY 10017, USA

Routledge is an imprint of the Taylor & Francis Group, an informa business

Copyright © 2002 by Barry Mason, Alice Sawyerr,
& the Institute of Family Therapy

Foreword copyright © 2002 by Nancy Boyd-Franklin

The rights of the editors and contributors to be identified as the authors of this work have been asserted in accordance with §§ 77 and 78 of the Copyright Design and Patents Act 1988.

All rights reserved. No part of this book may be reprinted or reproduced or utilised in any form or by any electronic, mechanical, or other means, now known or hereafter invented, including photocopying and recording, or in any information storage or retrieval system, without permission in writing from the publishers.

Notice:
Product or corporate names may be trademarks or registered trademarks, and are used only for identification and explanation without intent to infringe.

British Library Cataloguing in Publication Data
A C.I.P. for this book is available from the British Library
   ISBN 9781855752900 (pbk)

Edited, designed, and produced by Communication Crafts

CONTENTS

SERIES EDITORS' FOREWORD	vii
ABOUT THE AUTHORS	ix
FOREWORD *by Nancy Boyd-Franklin*	xiii
INTRODUCTION	xvii

PART I: Addressing the context

1 "Race", ethnicity, and child welfare
   Ravinder Barn   3

PART II: Theoretical perspectives

2 Culture, self, and cross-ethnic therapy
   Kwame Owusu-Bempah   19

3 Uncertainty, risk-taking, and ethics in therapy
   Inga-Britt Krause   34

PART III: **Practice perspectives**

4 Ethnic sameness and difference
   in family and systemic therapy
   Lennox K. Thomas — 49

5 The African Families Project: a black and white issue
   Amma Anane-Agyei, Wendy Lobatto, & Philip Messent — 69

6 "Strangers in foreign lands"
   Jocelyn Avigad & Jane Pooley — 82

7 Visible differences: individual and collective
   risk-taking in working cross-culturally
   Shila Khan — 95

8 A risky balance: striving to merge
   professional white issues and personal black issues
   Gella Richards — 111

PART IV: **Personal and professional development perspectives**

9 Getting it right, getting it wrong: developing
   an internal discourse about ethnicity and difference
   Gill Gorell Barnes — 133

10 Risky business: the rewards and demands
   of cross-cultural working with colleagues
   Liz Burns & Charmaine Kemps — 148

REFERENCES — 163
INDEX — 177

SERIES EDITORS' FOREWORD

As the Series Editors, we hope that our series has become known for, among other things, the presentation of new and challenging ideas. This book, however, raises the crucial and uncomfortable question, "Are we allowed to challenge some ideas but not others?" and the subsidiary question, "What makes it possible to challenge another person's ideas?"—for the book is written in the shadow of political correctness. It comments on the constraining effects of political correctness but goes a step further to propose ways in which we can transcend that position to have discussions about differences. It proposes that we don't have to play safe: we can take risks, if we first establish underlying respect for others' points of view. This book is about how we can understand each other better within and across cultural and ethnic differences.

The book was inspired by a recent conference, entitled "Exploring the Unsaid", organized by the Institute of Family Therapy in London, which gathered people from various ethnic, professional, and institutional backgrounds to share their experiences of trying to develop services and communicate across cultural boundaries. The enthusiasm of the participants led the editors of the book, Barry Mason and Alice Sawyerr, to compile prominent papers from this conference into one volume, which not only increases the impact of these ideas but extends them to a wider public.

Therapists in the UK, particularly those in urban areas, are working increasingly with clients who come from cultures different from their own, and they therefore find it difficult to know how to conduct therapy in a respectful and helpful way. We cannot assume that all our clients share our most basic assumptions about "what family relations should be" and "the appropriate role for a therapist". This book introduces the voices of authors from many cultures, so the reader has a chance both to learn about many different assumptions and to hear people describe the process of trying to communicate across their differences. The authors have not played safe: they have taken risks and written from very personal experiences, and we are grateful to them for opening the first phase of a dialogue with our readers.

David Campbell
Ros Draper
London, 2002

ABOUT THE AUTHORS

The Editors

Barry Mason is white British. He is the Director of the Institute of Family Therapy, London, and is well known for his contribution to the development of family therapy training in the United Kingdom. He has contributed to numerous books and journals and has recently completed co-editing (with David Campbell) a book on supervision as well as writing up research on chronic pain and relationships.

Alice Sawyerr is African Canadian. Her background training is in psychology, social work, and family therapy. She is a full-time clinician at the Marlborough Family Service in St John's Wood, London, a child, family, and all-age assessment and treatment mental health service. She lectures part-time in Family and Systemic Therapy at Royal Holloway, University of London, and in Counselling Psychology at the University of Surrey Roehampton, London. She also teaches at the Institute of Family Therapy, London. She is currently a PhD student at the University of London, where her research interest includes the development of ethnicity in pre-schoolers.

ABOUT THE AUTHORS

The Contributors

Amma Anane-Agyei, Social Worker, Tower Hamlets Social Services, London.

Jocelyn Avigad, Principal Family Therapist, the Medical Foundation for the Care of Victims of Torture, London.

Ravinder Barn, Senior Lecturer in Applied Social Studies, Royal Holloway, University of London.

Liz Burns, Family Therapist, Aylesbury Child & Family Psychiatric Service.

Gill Gorell Barnes, Honorary Senior Lecturer, Tavistock Clinic, London; Family Therapist, Supervisor and Family Researcher and formerly Consultant for Training, Institute of Family Therapy, London.

Charmaine Kemps, Senior Family Therapist, Department of Child and Adolescent Psychiatry, Milton Keynes.

Shila Khan, Systemic Psychotherapist, Redbridge Health Care, London.

Inga-Britt Krause, Training and Development Consultant with Black and Minority Ethnic Communities, Tavistock Clinic, London.

Wendy Lobatto, Family Therapist in Child & Adolescent Mental Health Team Community Health, Sheffield.

Philip Messent, Social Work Manager, Tower Hamlets Social Services, London.

Kwame Owusu-Bempah, Reader in Psychology, School of Social Work, University of Leicester.

Jane Pooley, Freelance Organizational Consultant and Systemic Psychotherapist, Hertfordshire.

Gella Richards, Childhood Counselling Psychologist and Lecturer, University of Surrey Roehampton.

Lennox K. Thomas, Family and Individual Therapist in Private Practice, London.

The Institute of Family Therapy

The Institute of Family Therapy (IFT) was founded in 1977 under its first Chair of Council, the late Dr Robin Skynner. Over the last 25 years it has become well known for its training courses (from introductory to doctoral level) and its clinical work, including its mediation service. It has a membership of nearly 200 senior practitioners based all over the United Kingdom and beyond. The Institute has always sought to initiate new developments in response to emerging needs, and in this respect it has recently established the Centre for Child Focused Practice. The President of the Institute is Yasmin Alibhai-Brown, MBE.

Further information about the Institute of Family Therapy can be obtained from:

The Institute of Family Therapy
24–32 Stephenson Way
London NW1 2HX

tel: 44 (0)20 7391 9150
fax: 44 (0)20 7391 9169
email: ift@psyc.bbk.ac.uk
web page: www.instituteoffamilytherapy.org.uk

FOREWORD

Nancy Boyd-Franklin
Professor of Psychology, Graduate School of Applied
and Professional Psychology, Rutgers University, New Jersey

It is an honour and a privilege to write the foreword to this pioneering book. The editors and contributing authors, through their courage and willingness to take risks, have modelled for all of us the future direction of the mental health and family therapy fields. This book, written in the twenty-first century at the intersection of the modern and the postmodern era, challenges all of us to think creatively about our cross-cultural practice. It represents both an evolution in the field of cross-cultural treatment and a revolutionary opportunity to view the dilemmas of this work through the straightforward and insightful dialogue of its authors. Through their innovative work, they have successfully framed cross-cultural issues as central to the professional ethics of good practice for the entire field, rather than as a tangential issue for marginalized groups.

This book makes a powerful contribution on four levels:

1. our cross-cultural work with clients;
2. the necessity to do ongoing, thorough self-examination in order to understand our own cultural influences and biases;

3. the need for cross-cultural dialogue between professional colleagues to facilitate effective working relationships;
4. the dynamics of institutional racism and organizational change.

On the first level—that is, that of cross-cultural work with clients—this book expands our conceptual as well as our practice framework. The authors call upon us to begin by viewing all therapeutic work as a negotiation or an exchange of values and cultures between the therapist and the client. This prototype allows us to view knowledge of a particular group metaphorically as a camera lens, which must be adjusted for each new client with whom we work. This paradigmatic shift effectively transports us beyond the rigid frame of cultural stereotypes to the freeing postmodern conceptualization of creative conversations between the therapist and the client about cultural issues. This powerful and hopeful approach opens the door for therapists of all cultures to develop cultural competency and to embrace—rather than withdraw from—the dilemmas of this work.

The authors of this volume have challenged all of us to view the differences and similarities between cultures from an assumption of equality and normality rather than hierarchy and pathology. They have questioned practice based exclusively on Western professional views and have encouraged the mental health field to expand its theoretical models to include non-Western cultural beliefs and practices. Through their thoughtful and insightful work, they have given voice to aspects of ethnic-minority cultures that are often overlooked by mainstream therapeutic approaches. A wide range of cross-cultural issues are presented, including: the differences between "collectivistic" cultures and the more "individualistic" aspects of Western culture; extended kinship roles; beliefs about health and mental health; spirituality and religion; and the importance of family connections and obligations. Perhaps even more importantly, this book has placed the spotlight on areas often avoided by the mental health field, such as the effects of racism, poverty, and sexism on our clients' lives. These clinicians model for all of us a respect for their clients and a sincere belief in what one group of authors has termed the parents' "good intentions" for their children. This emphasis on positive connotation and reframing is often the crucial element in the ability of therapists to join effectively with clients from cultural groups, who often approach health and mental health systems with fear, mistrust, and "healthy cultural suspicion". The wonderful clinical cases and vignettes throughout the book graphically illustrate these points and greatly enrich the experience for all readers.

The second level at which this book speaks to all of us is in its emphasis on the need for an examination of our own backgrounds, beliefs, cultural expectations, internalized racism, and understanding of what constitutes health and pathology. While this practice has been recommended for clinicians for some time, these authors have taken a major step forward by effectively demonstrating the process of introspection necessary for this difficult task to occur. By modelling a level of personal self-exploration and risk-taking, which has been very rare in the literature on cross-cultural treatment, they have led us on the difficult but rewarding journey that must occur if we are to be effective therapists. The authors caution us to be aware of our own countertransference when working with clients and families from our own cultural group as well as in our cross-cultural work.

The third area is one of the most innovative in this book. Through a series of personal vignettes, anecdotes, and reflecting-team dialogues, a number of the authors have taken the revolutionary step of exploring the challenges and dilemmas of mixed team work and of mental health professionals from different cultures working together to improve culturally competent service delivery. This work is truly groundbreaking and constitutes one of the "unsaid" secrets in our field. Their honest presentation of their struggle encourages us all to avoid the temptation to retreat into the "comfort of sameness" and to avoid that which is different or unknown. Ironically, this is often a parallel process, for if we retreat from the challenges of cross-cultural collegial and professional dialogue, we may miss an important opportunity to learn from each other and, ultimately, better to understand our clients and ourselves. This book provides a forum for a discussion and debate about these issues that are so often avoided in the field. As systems thinkers, we are once again reminded about the ways in which our own feelings of isolation, anger, fury, impotence, and fear of confronting our own beliefs and those of our colleagues are often a mirror of our clients' experiences.

Finally, this book challenges all of us to work towards institutional and organizational change. In their frank discussions, many of the authors have focused on institutional racism and the many levels of racial tension between systems and clients and between co-workers from different cultural and racial groups. These courageous clinicians have taken the risk of documenting their own experiences and their attempts and strategies for producing organizational change within their own mental health institutions and agencies. They have recognized the need for multi-systemic communication between mental health and social service agencies in order to ensure that empowerment and positive change occurs for our clients.

This book provides hope and strategic interventions for clinicians—not only in the United Kingdom, but in the United States and other countries—who are struggling to produce institutional, systemic change and are feeling overwhelmed by the process. It provides inspiration that can refuel, re-energize, and empower all of us to use our own creativity and to take the risks to produce change for our clients and for ourselves in our cross-cultural work.

INTRODUCTION

Michael Lerner, an American Jewish writer, Rabbi, and civil rights activist, and Cornel West, a leading African-American academic, Baptist minister, and professor of African-American studies and the philosophy of religion at Harvard University, wrote a best-selling book in 1995 called *Jews and Blacks*. The book comprises conversations, often blunt and hard hitting, between two long-standing friends and covers a range of issues including white racism, Jewish racism, black anti-Semitism, cultural identity and whiteness, and sexuality and ideas for reconciliation between different cultural groups. The book is a dialogue between very close friends who have created a context for challenging each other without undermining core mutual respect. Most of all, their book is about taking risks, of exploring the unsaid, of finding ways to go beyond safe discourses, particularly the safe discourses of political correctness.

Purpose of this book

This book, through its wide range of chapters, seeks to encourage the reader to speak the unsaid. It is important in any therapeutic work to always be asking the question of oneself, "What issues am I pulling back from addressing or avoiding in my work with clients, with colleagues, and with wider systems, and how do I explain to myself that I am doing this? Is it appropriate that I do not explore the unsaid at this point, or is it that I am not being brave enough to take a risk?" Of course, part of the reason why people may not take risks is because the context (e.g. the work place) does not provide a secure-enough base (Byng-Hall, 1995), personally and organizationally, to do so.

What this book does, through the various chapters in the four parts, is to provide the reader with a rich vein of ideas for taking risks, exploring the unsaid, and developing useful frameworks for addressing same-culture and cross-cultural issues.

Background to the book

During the past decade there has been an unprecedented growth in family therapy conferences and workshops focusing on race, culture, and ethnic identities. In 1991, the Trancultural Psychiatry Society (U.K.) and the Institute of Family Therapy, London, jointly presented a conference in London entitled, "Working with Families in a Multi-ethnic Society: Confronting Racism and Taking Account of Culture". This well-attended and successful conference led to further joint conferences in 1995 and 1997. A core group of practitioners—Gella Richards, Shila Khan, Maire Stedman, Gwynneth Down, and Alice Sawyerr, later joined by Jocelyn Avigad, Sue Fyvel, and Barry Mason—planned the November 1999 conference that inspired and gave name to this book. In considering the theme of the conference, there was agreement that we needed to explore the processes by which practitioners took risks and explored their dilemmas in developing creative cross-cultural therapeutic work. This theme had emerged from noticing the processes that we as a group were experiencing. We had begun to take more risks among ourselves, and this has been the more so since the conference took place. We could hardly present a conference on exploring the unsaid if we ourselves were not exploring it with each other. So a group consisting of a British black female, a British Asian female, a white Irish female, a white British female, an African Canadian female, a white South African Jewish female, a white British Jewish female, and a white British male has been meeting for four years. For its members, the group had become the major or only forum in which senior practitioners from multicultural, multi-ethnic backgrounds and from a variety of institutions have been able to meet to talk about their practice in working cross-culturally and with the same culture, without having to be too mindful of offending others. Most have said that they can ask questions about each other and take the kind of risk that they feel they might avoid taking in their own organizations. In particular, a level of trust has been developed between the members of the group that has allowed us to facilitate this process.

Some of the issues recently discussed in the group have been: institutional racism and our personal and organisational relationships to it; our views as to the implications for white practitioners if ethnic-minority practitioners are employed mainly to work with their own culture; the need for white, not just ethnic-minority, professionals to explore in detail how they work cross-culturally and for both to explore the dilemmas that each experiences when working cross-culturally; our views in relation to when an accepted practice in one culture might be seen as disrespectful or oppressive in another culture. An example would be when men in some cultures will not shake hands with women because, for a variety of reasons, their religion restricts cross-sex touching. The exploration of these issues and others, such as the way we use language, is part of a culture within the group of being able to ask, be curious, about any issue without fear of being "outed" as racist or oppressive.

The discussions that have taken place in the group, particularly since the conference, have been both tense, refreshing, and exciting. We have all taken risks because we realize that to develop a better understanding between our different cultures and ethnicities we cannot play safe. We (the editors) take the view that to develop intimacy, to develop closeness of whatever kind, one has to be prepared to take chances and risk vulnerability. We could, indeed, play safe and say "the right thing", but this is what we think people in the helping professions already do too often. Based on our positive group experience, we would suggest that, where possible, readers consider forming the kind of multicultural, multi-ethnic group that we have been part of and have found so useful. It is important, however, that in forming such a group careful consideration is given to issues such as confidentiality and the boundaries between personal and professional issues. A careful balance needs to be struck through negotiation between group members to facilitate the creation of a context for encouraging individuals to take risks while ensuring that its minority members are not subjected to new or further oppressive practices by silencing them within the group. This is not to say that all group members shouldn't be challenged (and, indeed, this is what happens in practice) but the challenges should come from a position of integrity rather than from a lack of integrity.

The structure of the book

One particular contribution of this volume lies in its assembly of a multicultural and multiracial team of practitioners, academics, and researchers who have taken risks rather than played safe. The authors acknowledge their assumptions and take positions while remaining open to the diverse interests of their intended readers. As Nancy Boyd-Franklin rightly emphasizes in her Foreword to this book, they share commitments to frame cross-cultural issues as central to the professional ethics of good practice in the field of mental health. While the majority of the contributors are family therapists, the disciplines of sociology (Ravinder Barn), psychology (Kwame Owusu-Bempah, Gella Richards), social work (Amma Anane-Agyei), and anthropology (Inga-Britt Krause) are also represented.

It is perhaps an overused cliché to say that the future lies with our children. However, in a book that deals with the effects of marginalization, it is important that in the chapter by Ravinder Barn, which forms the first of the four parts into which the book is divided, children are placed centre stage in setting the context, not least because in developments in systemic thinking and practice, children have often been marginalized. In the second part, on theory, Kwame Owusu-Bempah and Inga-Britt Krause provide a richness of thought about theory and begin to show how some of these ideas can be used in practice. The third part, on practice, looks at how creative risk-taking has been translated into practice. The authors—Lennox K. Thomas, Amma Anane-Agyei, Wendy Lobatto, Philip Messent, Jocelyn Avigad, Jane Pooley, Shila Khan, Gella Richards—not only describe and analyse their work but do so by highlighting their dilemmas and how they have addressed these dilemmas as part of the development of effective practice. The final part of the book, with chapters by Gill Gorell Barnes, Liz Burns, and Charmaine Kemps, deals with personal and professional development issues through an emphasis on self-reflexivity and the sharing of an openness and vulnerability. The authors look at family history, culture, and the beliefs that have informed their personal lives and professional work. Some attention is also given to how colleagues have addressed the tensions and difficulties of their working relationships and the impact on, and from, their organizations.

The writers of the chapters in this book at times share the rawness of their emotions (such as the hurt, the frustration, the pain), their wisdom and hope, and the struggle that is part and parcel of dealing with institutional racism and organizational change. In the wake of the Macpherson Inquiry Report (1999), and its recommendations, on the murder of the London teenager Stephen Lawrence as a result of a racist attack by young white men, this book is a contribution to ways in which practitioners in mental health and allied fields can work towards diminishing intentional and unintentional forms of discrimination and institutional racism.

Conclusion

One of the central notions of utilizing a systemic approach is the importance of constructively engaging with difference, as well as with similarity. We believe that if professionals do not constructively engage with difference—and by this we mean from an assumption of equality and non-pathology—we significantly lessen the chances of developing creative ways of working with people both within and across cultures. We also believe that engaging with difference enables us to explore the ties that bind as well as the binds that separate. Thus, by exploring the unsaid we hope that practitioners will be enabled to develop greater cultural competency and thus play a positive role in eradicating racism and promoting and valuing diversity. We have very much enjoyed the experience of putting together this book as it has not only provided us with opportunities to learn from each other, but also to learn about ourselves and reflect on our practice and our relationships with colleagues. We would be very happy to hear from readers about the contribution the book makes in the pursuit of developing more effective and creative cross-cultural practice

Acknowledgement Our thanks to Juliet Carr, at the Institute of Family Therapy, for her valuable contribution in helping us with some of the administrative aspects of editing this book.

Barry Mason
Alice Sawyerr

PART I

ADDRESSING THE CONTEXT

CHAPTER 1

"Race", ethnicity, and child welfare

Ravinder Barn

The racial and cultural heterogeneity of Britain remains the subject of much debate and discussion. Terms such as multiracial and multicultural are employed without any consensual framework about the ways in which diversity could or should be sustained and developed. Moreover, the contested nature of concepts such as multiculturalism and ethnicity ensures fragmented thinking. The corollary of this is that within public and social policy, such fragmentation leads to disparate, often weak, strategies and approaches in meeting the needs of minority ethnic groups.

Minority ethnic groups, according to the last census in 1991, constituted 5.5% of the total population in Britain. Minority ethnic children constituted about 9% of the total child population. Overall, there are about a million children from a minority ethnic background in Britain. While many of the minority ethnic children will grow up to lead emotionally secure and healthy lives, a certain proportion will come to the attention of health and social services as a result of ill-health, poverty, poor housing/homelessness, racial discrimination and disadvantage, and family dysfunctionality. This chapter focuses on the disadvantaged and vulnerable children who come to the attention of social and mental health services.

The chapter provides an understanding of some of the important issues and concerns facing minority ethnic families and children in Britain today. It places a particular focus on risk and vulnerability and on the child welfare system. It is argued that a sophisticated understanding of the heterogeneity of the minority ethnic population is vital. Moreover, there is a need for the revision of social welfare theoretical and practice wisdom.

Background

There are 50,000 children "looked after" in England, and about 32,000 who are considered to be "at risk" and placed on the social services child-protection register. (The term "looked after" refers to children in local authority care who are accommodated with parental or child consent and those in care following court proceedings. The terms "in care", and "in the public care system" are often used interchangeably.) Due to the lack of statistical recording and collation in any systematic way, the proportion of minority ethnic children within the care system and on the child-protection register remains unknown.

Previous research has pointed to the low levels of adequate and appropriate services to meet the needs of minority ethnic families and children on the part of social services (Ahmed et al., 1986; Barn, 1993; Caesar, Parchment, & Berridge, 1994; Cheetham, 1981a). Moreover, the numbers of minority ethnic children have been shown to be high in the public care system. Some early research in the mid-1950s carried out by the National Children's Home (1954) initiated concern about the plight of minority children in the care system and identified practice considerations. As the significant arrival of minority ethnic groups from South Asia and the Caribbean began in the mid-to late 1950s and 1960s, it is possible that some of these minority children in public care in the early 1950s included "war babies". These war babies were mixed-parentage children born of white mothers and African-American GI fathers during the Second World War (Baker, 1999).

In 1958, during the assimilationist period, the Family Welfare Association reported that the problems of minority families were no different from those of the indigenous population and that these families were making adequate use of services. Subsequent studies highlighted the problem of a growing number of minority ethnic children in residential homes and the difficulties of finding substitute families for these children (Fitzherbert, 1967; Rowe & Lambert, 1973). During the 1970s, models of multiculturalism and ethnic sensitivity emerged in which it was held that an understanding of minority cultures was important in attempting to meet their needs. Such thinking, albeit well-intentioned, led to the black family becoming the focus of attention (often negatively), resulting in some commentators stating that the black family had become pathologized (Carby, 1982; Lawrence, 1981). The extent to which the antiracist thinking of the 1980s, with its emphasis on institutional racism, helped to shift away from the deficit model of the black family is arguable.

Empirical research in the area of child welfare, over the last twelve years, has continued to show the extent to which the black family is disadvantaged. The situation of the different minority ethnic groups has been documented. For example, it has been shown that children of African-Caribbean, and mixed Caribbean/white, parentage are much more likely to be in the care system than are other minority ethnic groups (Barn, 1993; Barn, Sinclair, & Ferdinand, 1997). Research evidence also shows that these groups are likely to be referred by statutory agencies and are susceptible to entering the public care system at times of crisis (Barn, 1993; Barn et al., 1997; Bebbington & Miles, 1989; Rowe, Hundleby, & Garnett, 1989). It would appear that such crisis situations lead to rapid entry into care, suggesting low levels of preventive help.

The disadvantage experienced by African-Caribbean children and young people has been highlighted. Barn et al. (1997) found that African-Caribbean children were twice more likely to enter care, in the early stages, compared to their white counterparts. They were also more likely than white children to spend longer periods in care. Barn et al. (1997) documented that 1 in 3 looked-after African-Caribbean children remained in the care system for more than five years compared to 1 in 10 white children.

The high rate of entry into care of some minority ethnic children, and their subsequent experiences in the care system, have been the focus of policy and practice considerations over the last four decades. Much of the debate has been politicized in terms of multiculturalism, racial harmony, and ethnic identity. Nowhere is this more apparent than in the field of fostering and adoption. Issues and concerns arising from these situations as they relate to social-work assessment of children's needs and parental capabilities are discussed below.

Research studies over the last forty years have continued to document racial disadvantage and discrimination among minority ethnic groups in a number of areas, including housing, education, health, criminal justice, employment, and the personal social services. Moreover, the impact of racist immigration laws has served to ensure the division of families across continents, leading to further hardship and emotional turmoil.

It is important to note that although collective nouns such as "black", "Asian", minority ethnic, and non-white are employed by academics, policy makers, and practitioners to refer to a certain section of the population, such terms should not be taken to imply homogeneity in cultural and/or racial experiences in Britain. Careful reading of research studies shows that an understanding of the differential experiences of minority ethnic groups is crucial (Modood et al., 1997). Such understanding leads to a conceptual framework that can encompass the complexity of variables such as "race", ethnicity, religion, class, gender, disability, and sexual orientation. Thus, a multidimensional framework is envisioned leading to better and improved assessments and interventions.

Some questions needing urgent consideration by researchers, policy makers, and practitioners

- Why are some minority children highly represented in the care system?
- What work is done with families pre- and post-admission into care, and how effective is it?
- What are the particular needs and concerns of looked-after minority children, and how are these met?

- What are the relative advantages/disadvantages of "same-race" and transracial placements for children?
- What works in leaving care preparation in relation to minority ethnic children's needs and concerns?

Social-work policy and practice

Much of the early social-work research adopted a problematic approach and focused on minority family structures and lifestyles to understand the situation of these families (Fitzherbert, 1967; McCulloch, Batta, & Smith, 1979). The multicultural paradigm within research had an impact on practice. It appears that that there was little or no attempt to explore the impact of structural racism on minority family life, and the relevance or appropriateness of British social-work theory and practice. It is unfortunate that the negative overemphasis on minority family structures and lifestyles has led to a paradigm of deficit within the helping professions which is now in need of a major and significant challenge (Barn, 2000; Rashid & Rashid, 2000; Small, 1984).

Assessment

How does the assessment process take into account the "race" and ethnicity context of the client? Social-work theory and practice has been much, and often rightly, maligned for neglecting to incorporate the "race" dimension.

In a recent paper, Dutt and Phillips (2000) highlight the importance of a holistic framework encompassing "race" and ethnicity alongside other variables to make comprehensive assessments of black families and children. They argue that Western theoretical frameworks—for example, attachment theory—are applicable to all human relationships but must be adapted for their applicability to black families. For instance, the key role played by differing family structures, communities, and support networks in forming important and multiple attachments requires attention (Thomas, 1996).

Are social workers and others in the helping professions consciously exercising overt discriminatory behaviour?

Research studies have documented that social workers and others in the helping professions may or may not be overtly racist, but that due to institutional racism and negative racial stereotypes, the black family is pathologized. Negative thinking feeds into policy and practice, leading to discriminatory behaviour and poor outcomes for black families (Barn, 1993; Johnson, 1986; Kornreich et al., 1973).

In a study of six local authorities in and around London and the Midlands, Gibbons et al. (1995) found that while the proportion of minority ethnic children was not inconsistent with their representations in the local population, they were overrepresented among referrals for physical abuse compared to white (58% compared to 42%), and underrepresented among referrals for sexual abuse (20% compared to 31%). The researchers also highlighted ethnic and cultural differences in forms of punishment. That is, minority ethnic families were more often referred for using an implement, such as a cane, than were white families. It was found that 43% of Africans, 40% of Asians, and 30% of African Caribbeans had beaten their children with a stick or other implement, compared with 16% of whites. Differences in referral agencies and their concerns regarding black and white families have been documented elsewhere (Barn, 1993; Barn et al., 1997). It should be noted that Gibbons and her colleagues (1995) documented that "the consequences of the injuries inflicted on black and Asian children were no more likely to be long-lasting" and that it was "the form the punishment took that was unacceptable to community agents who referred these children" (p. 40).

A study of three local authorities in London and the Midlands found a high proportion of minority ethnic children on the child-protection register—60% compared to 40% white (Barn et al., 1997). It was also found that minority ethnic children were more likely to be referred for physical injury than were their white counterparts, and less likely to be referred for sexual abuse. The group most highly represented from within the minority ethnic communities was Asian: 28% of the children were Asian, compared to 14% of African-Caribbean background and 14% of mixed parentage. This study highlighted the contested nature of the concepts of abuse and neglect within the context of the differing perceptions of black and white practitioners and birth parents around what constitutes "significant harm". Both the Gibbons and the Barn studies point to the social construction of abuse and neglect and to the fine line between "appropriate punishment" and "significant harm" (Gibbons et al., 1995; Barn et al., 1997). Moreover, our attention is drawn not only to the task of parenting in multiracial Britain, but also to the racialized judgements and approval of child welfare professionals and others.

It would appear that negative stereotypes about black families lead to certain common-sense wisdoms that perpetuate pernicious practice. Child abuse and neglect and child sexual abuse occur in all cultures, and all social class backgrounds. It is sometimes said that there is a veil of silence regarding child sexual abuse in black communities. However, child sexual abuse is taboo in all cultures, and consequently open discussion of such a topic remains taboo in all families. Daily racial-discrimination experiences by black families lead them to be cautious of externally organized statutory or voluntary help. Thus, it is possible that needs and concerns remain hidden to a far greater degree than in the white communities.

Some other areas of concern identified in qualitative research into "race" and child protection include the complex process of using interpreters and how families may be disadvantaged in the process; a lack of holistic approach to assessment and case planning; and the mental and physical health of parents (Chand, 2000; Dutt & Phillips, 1996; Humphries, Atkar, & Baldwin, 1999). Research is needed into these areas as well as the general notion of "good-enough parenting" in multiracial Britain.

An overemphasis on certain areas, such as black families' methods of punishment and child-rearing, diverts attention away from other aspects that are significant in the lives of black children. For example, minority ethnic children and their families are subject to racial harassment, racial discrimination, and/or institutional racism. Although racism causes significant harm, it is not, in itself, a category of abuse. The experience of racism is likely to affect the responses of the child and family to the enquiry and assessment process. Failure to protect children from racism will further undermine the efforts to protect them from other forms of significant harm. The effects of racism differ for different communities and individuals and cannot be assumed.

Residential and substitute family care of minority ethnic children raises many important issues, including emotional/psychological needs and the "lived experience" that should give a positive affirmation of the child's racial and cultural background in a "race"-conscious society.

Research studies over the years have pointed to the difficulties of finding appropriate substitute family placements for black children and have shown black children to be "hard to place" in family settings (Rowe & Lambert, 1973). The realization of the negative effects of transracial placements (Divine, 1983; Gill & Jackson, 1983; Small, 1984) contributed to changes in child care legislation to consider the racial and ethnic background of children looked after.

The 1989 Children Act, Section 22(5)(c), identified the importance of four elements:

- "Race"
- Culture
- Religion
- Language

The implementation of these considerations by local-authority social services departments has been varied. The author's own research in this area has shown that where local authorities have invested adequate resources, certain minority-ethnic-group children (African-Caribbean, and Asian) have a good chance of being placed in foster-family settings and, more specifically, in families that reflect the child's own racial and cultural background (Barn, 1993; Barn et al., 1997). However, it appears that there are, at times, crude attempts at racial matching as a result of a lack of comprehensive assessment of the child's needs and concerns. As a consequence, some minority ethnic foster-carers find themselves placed in difficult situations where they are given little preparation and support. Such practice does not lend itself to the retention of foster-carers, and it creates problems in meeting placement needs. A recent study by the Family Rights Group has documented the continual practice of transracial placements by local authorities and ad hoc progress in equal-opportunity and anti-discriminatory matters (Richards & Ince, 2000).

Barn et al. (1997) found that mixed-parentage children present a placement dilemma for social services. The vast majority of mixed-parentage children who enter the care system come from single-parent families: birth mothers are white, and the fathers, who are African-Caribbean, are in most cases not in the picture. The mixed-parentage children may have little or no contact with their black relatives. There is currently little research evidence available about the formal and informal support networks of lone white mothers. There is clearly a need for helping agencies to operate within a supportive framework to obviate the admission of these children into the care system. With regard to substitute placements, Barn et al. (1997) documented that mixed-parentage children were equally likely to be placed with a black or a white family. It was of concern to note that some placement decisions were being made within a framework of biological notions of "race" and colour, and there was a lack of comprehensive assessment of need.

Intervention

The link between assessment and intervention is an important one. It is well recognized that mutually consensual goals and objectives lead to appropriate interventions and positive outcomes. The question that has to be asked is: "Does intervention lead to positive outcomes for minority ethnic families and children?" Clearly, the social services have a role to play in helping families in crisis, protecting children from harm, and ensuring that their intervention is in the best interest of the child and family. The extent to which universalist provision helps or hinders black families is discussed elsewhere (Barn, 1998). The need for appropriate and adequate assessment and intervention and service provision has been documented since the influential studies of Juliet Cheetham over two decades ago (Cheetham, 1981a, 1981b, 1982).

There is evidence to suggest that family support remains underdeveloped with black families (Barn, 1993; Butt & Box, 1998;

Jones & Butt, 1995). Butt and Box (1998) documented the low level of minority ethnic attraction to family centres and found that "black communities do not always have access to family centres and rarely access the full range of services available" (p. 105). The low level of awareness of the availability of the range of services has also been documented by research studies (Barn et al., 1997; Butt & Box, 1998; Qureshi, Berridge, & Wenman, 2000).

The need to develop family-focused methods of working has been highlighted as crucial (Barn et al., 1997). The extent to which education and training equip students in the helping professions to develop their skill and competence in engaging minority ethnic families is questionable (Penketh, 2000). Moreover, in some professions, it appears that there is little or no post-qualifying training to help practitioners consolidate their learning "on the job" (Barn et al., 1997).

In our national study, *Acting on Principle* (Barn et al., 1997), exploring the implementation of Section 22(5)(c) of the 1989 Children Act, we documented that practitioners found some family-oriented methods of working such as "family group working" to be useful in resolving cases of conflict between adolescents and their Asian parents. Other policy and practice mechanisms integrated within the process of assessment and intervention, such as specialist teams set up to advise and assist in antiracist practice, were considered by managers and practitioners to be useful. We also highlighted that issues and concerns around "race" and ethnicity had fallen off the social services agenda, particularly in one London local authority, which had prided itself on its equal-opportunities and antiracist stance in the 1980s.

It is important that all practitioners develop their skill and competence in working with minority ethnic birth and substitute families. Family-oriented approaches, as well as direct work with youngsters in the care system, need to be developed and tailored in flexible ways to meet the needs of diverse groups. There is a growing literature in the area of "race", ethnicity, and social welfare. An appropriate integration of research, theory, and practice is required to begin to meet the needs of minority ethnic children and families.

There is some research evidence about the quality of foster placements in relation to black children. Rowe et al. (1989) showed that mixed-parentage children were more likely to be in a placement that disrupted than were other black or white children. Some of the positive factors identified by researchers which may lead to stability and security for black children include regular contact with birth parents and/or siblings placed elsewhere, understanding and empathy from the foster-carer (Barn, 1993; Barn et al., 1997), and placement at a younger age and with a sibling (Rowe et al., 1989; Thoburn, Norford, & Rashid, 2000). Ince (1998) highlights the impact of transracial placements on black young people's racial identity. She found that five of the young people, in her sample of ten, perceived themselves to be white while growing up in care. Due to a lack of racial/cultural input from white foster/adoptive parents, and from social services, and a lack of contact with black people, these young people showed a resistance to "mixing" with black people and held negative views about them.

There is research literature from both the United States and Britain that shows that transracial placements can result in black children having a poor self-concept and a negative racial identity (Gill & Jackson, 1983; Simon & Alstein, 1981).

The difficulties faced by white substitute parents in ensuring that black children grow up in an environment in which they develop a positive sense of their own racial and cultural identity has been highlighted in the literature. A recent study into permanent family placements where two-thirds of the children were of mixed parentage has documented differences between black and white foster-carers (Thoburn et al., 2000). The study found that "whilst some white families can successfully parent children who are of a different ethnic origin from themselves, they have extra obstacles to surmount in ensuring that the young people have a positive sense of themselves as members of a particular ethnic group" (p. 159). In a study of the Post-Adoption Centre in London, Howe and Hinings (1987) found that white adoptive parents to black children tended to be overrepresented among those seeking help and advice. Clearly, these families recognized their own difficulties and were able and willing to seek external help. It is possible that there are other families in crisis who do not come to the attention of caring agencies. The extent to which the difficulties experienced by white adoptive and foster families looking after black children result in placement disruption is not known.

In their review on the outcome of transracial placements, Rushton and Minnis (2000) concluded that where transracial placements are the only option, then consideration needs to be given to placing children in multi-ethnic communities and that support and training should be provided for the substitute families.

In relation to residential care, Barn (1993) found that children placed in residential homes within their own multiracial, multicultural locality had a positive racial and ethnic identity as a result of regular contact with their own community, and birth family, and as a result of the positive influences made by black residential staff. In a study on racial identity attitudes and self-esteem among black (African-Caribbean) young people in residential care, and those in the community, Robinson (2000) found relatively high levels of self-esteem and internalization of (positive racial) attitudes. Robinson suggests that the predominance of such attitudes among young black people in residential care could be linked to the inner-city multiracial location of the residential homes and to the positive racial attitudes of their care workers, the majority of whom were black.

Ethnic monitoring

In terms of policy development, it has to be said that in the absence of local and national statistics, agencies are ill-equipped to plan and deliver appropriate services (Barn & Sinclair, 1999). In our 1997 study, *Acting on Principle*, we highlighted the need for appropriate management information systems and made a strong recommendation for central government to take a lead on this (Barn et al., 1997). Three years on, it is good to learn that the Department of Health will be collating information on ethnic origin of looked-after children.

The Children Act Report to Parliament declares that "ethnic monitoring will be introduced into routine statistical collections on children's services from the year 2000" (Department of Health, 2000, p. 6). It is encouraging to note that the government recognizes the policy and practice implications of such data collection, and it is to be hoped that such an exercise will not remain a mere data-gathering tool. The report informs us (p. 6) that

during 2000–2001, it will be possible to provide information on:
- How ethnicity is related to the reasons for children needing help from social services
- The actual services children from ethnic minorities receive and
- The associated expenditure

It is important to state that collation of information is not an end in itself. Appropriate action and service delivery are crucial. Management information systems have to be accountable and tied into appropriate targets and action.

Conclusion

This chapter has highlighted some areas of social-work practice that play a key role in the lives of minority ethnic families and children. While it is acknowledged that minority ethnic families may experience racial disadvantage and discrimination in a range of areas, it is argued that the helping professions need to develop a knowledge base that integrates research, theory, and practice within a multidimensional framework incorporating "race", ethnicity, social class, disability, religion, and other such areas. In the absence of such an approach, it is argued that practice remains ad hoc and poorly developed and serves to further disadvantage minority ethnic families and children.

PART II

THEORETICAL PERSPECTIVES

CHAPTER 2

Culture, self, and cross-ethnic therapy

Kwame Owusu-Bempah

Among ideas and practices that vary across cultural contexts are beliefs about health and responses to disease, and also perceptions of mental health and psychological well-being. This renders any attempt at a "universal" definition of health problematic, such as the World Health Organization's: "A state of complete physical, mental and social well-being and not merely the absence of disease or infirmity." This is an unrealistic state that any human adult or young person may be expected to maintain over time. Besides, spiritual well-being is missing from this definition despite its centrality and importance to conceptions of general well-being in most world cultures. Belief in mystical phenomena, in the influence of spirits or supernatural beings on a person's health or even destiny, is the commonest explanation of psychological problems throughout the world (Richeport-Haley, 1998). Consequently, Richeport-Haley advises, clinicians practising in multi-ethnic settings must be mindful that beliefs in spirit possession will be involved in some of the presenting problems of ethnic-minority clients.

Wijsen (1999) regards culture as the meaning system learned and shared by members of a group, and it is used by them to interpret experiences and to organize behaviour. This learned, shared and generationally transmitted meaning system encompasses ideas about health—including mental, emotional, spiritual, and psychological well-being. Every culture is a different world with its unique beliefs and psychology; so, at least, there are as many different worlds as there are religions and psychologies. Every religion has its cosmology, its own universe of reality, a unique set of concepts, images, a system of values, and a specific type of the perception of the world (Knappert, 1995; Lomov et al., 1993).

Hence, in the field of counselling and psychotherapy, Peavy (1996) recommends a radical new approach: that they be looked upon as forms of cultural practice rather than scientific undertaking and that, defined as cultural healing, mental health services need to be constructed more out of (1) "folk wisdom", (2) culturally sensible ways of communicating, (3) local rather than decontextualized knowledge, and (4) aspects of the knowledge developed through both scientific and humanistic research.

Culture and ethnicity

Therapy likely to meet these criteria requires an understanding of a given culture. Culture has been variously defined by the social-science disciplines. The consensus is that it is a composite structure of the real and the symbolic: beliefs, mythology, religion, ideas, sentiments, institutions, and objects transmitted generationally and internalized in varying degrees by its members. The culture of a given group is the sum of the shared ways of thought, reactions, rituals, customs, and habits or behaviour acquired directly or vicariously by its members. It includes child-rearing practices, kinship patterns, and beliefs about and reactions to health and disease—about physical and emotional health and medicine or healing. It also includes ethics governing interpersonal relationships. Artefacts aside, most of the elements of a culture are intangible, such as beliefs, values, and ideas that its members incorporate into their selfhoods; as such, they are a potent force in moulding and shaping their thoughts and conduct. In short, one's cultural background is hardly separable from one's psychological processes. Although a culture is shared by its members, each member experiences it in a unique way, resulting in individual personalities.

The terms "culture" and "ethnicity" (which nowadays seems to carry the same meaning as "race") are frequently used synonymously, but there is a conceptual distinction between the two, as the following definitions of ethnicity illustrate. Weidman (1978) views ethnicity as a "culturally transmitted meaning structure ... which can be determined by taking into consideration linguistic terms, marriage patterns, ethnic friendship networks, socialization in established ethnic enclaves, and self definition ..." (pp. 16–17). Montagu (1974) similarly describes an ethnic group as "one of a number of [human] populations ... which individually maintain their differences ... by means of isolating mechanisms such as geographic and social barriers ... an ethnic group may be a nation, a people, a language group, or a group bound together ... by a religion" (p. 186). An earlier definition of ethnicity by Morris (1968) portrays an ethnic group as a "distinct category of the population in a larger society whose culture is usually different from its own ... the members of such a group are, or feel themselves, or are thought to be bound together by common ties of race or nationality or culture" (p. 167).

These definitions imply that there is no single criterion by which an ethnic group can be defined. They show also that everyone belongs to not just one ethnic group; rather, we have multiple ethnicity in terms of geographical region, religion, social class, and so forth.

Individualism vs. collectivism

Attempts have been made to classify cultures according to whether they are collectivist (group-oriented) or individualist (individual-oriented). Triandis (1995) and other investigators (e.g. Markus & Kitayama, 1991) have suggested four attributes that distinguish collectivist cultures from individualist cultures. The following three are pertinent:

1. *The self.* Collectivist cultures define the self in terms of group-identity and interdependence with the members of one's group; individualist cultures conceive the self as autonomous and independent of groups.
2. *Setting goals.* In collectivist cultures, group goals have primacy over individual goals; individualists give priority to their personal goals.
3. *Meeting needs.* In collectivists cultures, members pay much attention to the needs of the group to which they belong. For example, if a relationship is desirable from the point of view of the group (e.g. the family), but costly from the point of view of the individual, the individual is likely to stay in the relationship. In contrast, individualists engage in exchange relationships ("What is in it for me?"), so that if the "costs" of being in a relationship exceed the benefits, individualists terminate the relationship.

These features indicate that cultures differ in their perception of the individual's relation to others. Triandis (1995) and others claim that, generally speaking, Western cultures are individualist. Some of the implications of cultural features for family therapy in multicultural settings will be discussed in later sections.

Other authors classify cultures in terms of their perception and use of time. For example, Hall (1983) and Levine and Bartlett (1984) distinguish between cultures that view time as a scarce commodity and cultures that view time as a limitless resource. Individualist cultures view time as a precious resource that must be rationed and controlled through the use of schedules and appointments. In contrast, time abounds in collectivist cultures; individuals have a flexible attitude to time, enabling them to service their various relationships and to meet their obligations to the various members of the community to whom they are bound. An obvious implication of this for therapy with individuals from collectivist cultural backgrounds is that strict adherence to schedules and appointments may impede therapy and may partly account for their reported reluctance to enter therapy and their high drop-out rates when they do so (e.g. Shiang et al., 1998).

Culture and the self

Psychotherapy, which often aims to increase self-awareness and self-efficacy, necessitates an understanding of the self. This can be enhanced by learning how other cultures perceive the self. Specifically the Western notion of the differentiated, autonomous self—of the individual as independent of one's environment and free from external or contextual control—is alien to most world cultures. Markus and Kitayama (1991) and Roland (1997) inform us that, within the context of world cultures, an actualized person is one who is most deeply connected to others and to society as a whole. There are the Pacific Island groups who view themselves not as bounded, distinct entities, but as integral pieces of an eternal scheme (Lesser, 1996). There are African cultures where one is less than human without "Us": the individual seeks the answer to the question, "Who am I?", not only in the question, "Who are we?", but in the question, "Who were we?" (including the living dead) (Mbiti, 1969; Holdstock, 2000; Owusu-Bempah & Howitt, 2000). In the extreme, there is the Innu culture, which does not even have a word for self-reference (Page & Berkow, 1991).

Naturally, the self does not manifest itself in the same form in all collectivist cultures. Nonetheless, the most common form it takes is that of social roles (Landrine, 1992). In collectivist cultures, a failure to perform one's role—for example, as spouse, mother, father, daughter, son, or grandparent, or even a friend—means a failure to be a person at all. Individuals do not have rights (to privacy, autonomy, and self-determination), but duties and obligations within the community to perform their roles well. Ho (1993) summarizes the self in collectivist cultures:

> The principles guiding social action are as follows: a) collective or group interests take precedence over those of individual, b) the fulfilment of external social obligations take precedence over the fulfilment of internal individual needs, and c) secur-

ing a place in the social order takes precedence over self-expression. [p. 250]

Regarding family function in collectivist cultures, one seeks to advance the family rather than the self; a member's concern is for the welfare and happiness of the family as a whole, including the extended family (which in some cases may be as "long as a piece of string").

Clinical practice with collectivist clients

Moghaddam (1993) questions seriously whether it is useful or desirable to export Western clinical services to traditional collectivist societies where there already exists traditional supportive psychologies, based mainly on indigenous religions and values. In other words, psychotherapy, as practised in the West, is virtually unknown and unnecessary in the majority of world cultures. Even in today's Western world, there are audible questions about the relevance of psychotherapy, based on Western views of "normal" development, experience, and behaviour, to diverse populations. For instance, Littlewood and Lipsedge (1989) question the applicability to other societies of European categories of mental illness. Fernando (1988) adds that current systems of classification, apart from overemphasizing pathology in thinking and behaviour, ignore the social, political, and economic factors that may cause, or at least contribute to, "illness". In like manner, Albee (1982) and other writers (e.g. Paniagua, 1994; Richeport-Haley, 1998) have pleaded for recognition of the role of poverty, meaningless work, unemployment, racism, and sexism (i.e. social inequalities) in producing psychopathology.

Yet others have gone further in warning that psychotherapy, like psychology, must seek to reflect the diversity of the populations it wishes to serve or perish. Otherwise, they argue, it will not only remain irrelevant to clients' needs, but will cease to be a viable professional resource to the majority of them (e.g. Hall, 1997; Huang, 1994; Landrine, 1992; Moncayo, 1998; Sue, 1987; Sue & Sue, 1999). To avoid this state of affairs, others (e.g. Richeport-

Haley, 1998; Shiang et al., 1998) have suggested incorporating specific cultural beliefs and behaviours into standard clinical treatments in order to make services to people from diverse backgrounds more relevant. A study conducted on the behalf of the Joseph Rowntree Foundation reinforces this suggestion. It demonstrates that ethnic-minority families in Britain who uphold collectivist values are the best able to cope with many social and personal problems (Hylton, 1997). Furthermore, they actually prefer solving problems for themselves than seeking help from voluntary or statutory agencies. The majority of the women interviewed had adapted to life in the United Kingdom yet preferred to stay within their own cultural traditions. So it might be that the lack of involvement of ethnic minorities in therapy and their speedier exit from therapy is a consequence of different cultural beliefs about normal experience or behaviour, or that their communities provide alternative services through family and community support. Exploring such possibilities would be more illuminating and fruitful than speculation.

In collectivist cultures, as we have seen, one seeks to advance the family rather than the self. The individual is changed, adjusted, and acted upon until she or he fits more harmoniously within the family, the relationship, or community, or the group changes to accommodate the individual in order to ensure the cohesiveness and survival of the family or group. That is, the self is nested within a larger self (e.g. the family) so that each strives to maintain a state of psychosocial homeostasis. Therapy based on these values is appropriate in this setting. Unfortunately, this sort of family is wrongly perceived by some professionals, including therapists and counsellors, who see some members of these families as submissive or passive. In such circumstances, assertiveness training is readily offered to the member perceived to be oppressed or enmeshed. This is inimical to therapeutic success since the family and its individual members function more as a single, integral unit (Maitra, 1996). Thus, Maitra warns, "practice, if based on Western (professional) views of 'normal' family function or child-rearing, can and does result in serious errors in assessment ... and makes 'therapeutic' interventions useless if not abusive in themselves" (p. 288). This is a signal that we must suspend our claims regarding the universality of Western definitions of "normal family", if by "universal" is meant "for all human groupings". It highlights the need for a wider knowledge-base about how families function.

Cultural competence

One common way of looking at the situation is to highlight therapists' poor knowledge and understanding of the cultures of their ethnic-minority clients (e.g. Sue & Sue, 1999). This presents us with the obvious solution of instigating initiatives designed to improve the cultural competence of practitioners. According to Sue and Sue (1999), a competent cross-cultural/ethnic practitioner possesses the cultural knowledge and linguistic skills to deliver effective interventions to members of that culture. Given such claims, and the preceding discussion, it is not surprising that issues of race, culture, and ethnicity often cause anxiety both in everyday social exchanges and in the activities of therapists (Leary, 1995). This is de-skilling and unhelpful, especially given the formidable task facing professionals in Western societies. Modern migratory patterns have ensured that almost every culture in the world is at least represented in any given country in the West (just as has happened in the reverse). The excessive demands that would be placed on any practitioner wishing to be competent to know something of the cultures of all sectors of the community can be illustrated, for example, by briefly examining language—one of the key aspects of any culture. Knappert (1995) estimates that more than a thousand different languages (not counting dialects) are spoken in Africa alone. No therapist could be expected to understand even just the beliefs and practices relating to health and illness, and the psychological functioning, of so many different cultures.

More pertinently, is cultural competence really an essential requirement or condition in the therapeutic relationship? Is it vital to an effective therapeutic outcome? Although a therapist may be knowledgeable about a particular culture or language, factors such as social class and status differential may also militate against therapeutic effectiveness (Hall, 1997; Fernando, 1988; O'Brian, 1990; Owusu-Bempah, 1997; Owusu-Bempah & Howitt, 2000). Even though cultural and language barriers can hamper cross-cultural/ethnic therapy, their removal or ethnic/cultural matching does not, in itself, ensure effective outcomes. The therapist's professional background and training, based on Western values and assumptions, such as those regarding the "normal" individual or "healthy" family, may offset any gains from ethnic matching, for example. Furthermore, the sharing of ethnicity by professionals and their clients does not always exclude the intrusion of crass stereotypes. For example, Hall (1997) recounts being approached by a black therapist who was treating a 5-year-old boy of "mixed-race" parentage (African/Japanese) who was showing inappropriate sexual behaviour at school. According to Hall, the therapist initially attributed the child's sexual misconduct to the stereotypical "heightened sexuality" of African-American males. The therapist was advised to investigate more extensively, and it emerged that the boy's mother was sexually abusing the child. Such abuse is a well-documented precursor to inappropriate sexual behaviour in children, so Hall asks: "Why then did the therapist assume a genetic cause in this case?" Hall's answer is: "not all the perpetrators of these cultural errors [racism] are White" (p. 645).

Indigenous therapies

Of course, there are training models (e.g. Parker, Moore, & Neimeyer, 1998) designed to remedy this sort of clinical work and prepare therapists, counsellors, and others for effective work with ethnic-minority clients. Characteristically, such training has been dominated by issues of "race" and culture. To reiterate, this can easily lead to feelings of insecurity among practitioners. Practitioners' sense of a lack of competence in matters of "race" and culture can make them feel de-skilled. Additionally, training programmes and practice that overemphasize ethnic/cultural issues can be criticized for lacking a clear conceptual framework and for trying to use simplistic and formulaic methods to solve complex structural problems (Cacas, 1984; Fernando, 1988; Owusu-Bempah, 1997; Owusu-Bempah & Howitt, 2000).

Among the possible solutions to some of the difficulties outlined above would be the development of interventions that are culturally diverse enough to be relevant to a wide variety of groups, regardless of racial and cultural/ethnic backgrounds. Needs to develop routes to cultural competence would lie in the development of indigenous therapies. Following Azuma's (1984) requirement that psychology needs to develop in a particular culture before it can be applied to that culture, indigenous (culture-specific) therapies would involve distinctive theories and practices for each cultural context. Foreign theories and research methods would be retained only if they were relevant to that particular cultural context.

Eco-system approach

"If one finger is sore, the whole hand will hurt."
Chinese proverb; quoted by Smith and Bond (1993, p. 119)

The "indigenous-therapies" approach within mainstream psychotherapy is less than completely practical. There is a monumental amount of work to be done, given institutional patterns of training professionals in psychological work and the limited resources devoted so far to developing indigenous therapies. A somewhat more practical approach for the meantime is the eco-system perspective, which manages to avoid some of the inherent difficulties of current approaches to cross-cultural/ethnic psychotherapy (Owusu-Bempah & Howitt, 2000). The key feature of the eco-system perspective is the individual's goodness-of-fit with his or her environment, an intimate interaction between individuals and his or her environment (Wakefield, 1996). A person forms a symbiotic relationship with their environment in which both are mutually influencing. In Wakefield's view, a therapeutic intervention based on the eco-system perspective begins with such questions as: "Is it more fruitful to study social behaviour by focusing on an individual's motivations and cognitions, or by examining the way social structures mould a person's behaviour and thought?" So, in the context of family therapy, the issue might be expressed as whether intervention should focus on an individual member(s), or on the whole family, or adopt a broader perspective to understanding and supporting the family.

Interaction at any point in the eco-system affects parts of the system. So, for some ethnic-minority families, the therapist might prefer to commence intervention with the neighbouring parts of the system in which, for example, the parent–child relationship is nested or embedded, such as grandparents or some other part of the extended family. We have already seen how, in collectivist or ethnic-minority communities, the kinship system or the extended family is the social and psychological locus throughout life for the majority of members of the community. Social, personal, economic, and status needs of the person are largely played out and fulfilled overwhelmingly within the extended family (Kakar, 1978; Roland, 1997). Treating some ethnic-minority clients in isolation is, therefore, a psychotherapeutic error (Landrine, 1992, Maitra, 1996). All of this follows from the repeated observation that the self in collectivist cultures is usually defined in terms of roles that exist for the good of one's group and not individuals.

Some of the major advantages of the eco-system approach (Wakefield, 1996) are:

- Helping practitioners see the interconnectedness between the individual and his or her environment that is involved in the individual's problem. The focus is removed from the individual onto the transaction between the individual and his or her environment. Thus, there is a dual concern in intervention which includes the individual but goes beyond the individual.
- It is a method of assessment that is both useful and comprehensive.
- It allows practitioners to employ appropriate domain-specific theories of intervention.
- The bias of practitioners towards individual-centred therapy becomes difficult to maintain.

Richeport-Haley (1998) provides a case study that illustrates the benefits of using a client's family and extended family as a resource:

> A young man in his 20s was court ordered to therapy for possession and dealing of marijuana. He would be imprisoned if this happened one more time. His mother, who spoke only Spanish, and the oldest son, who translated for her, came to therapy. The goal was to get the boy off marijuana. The intervention was to have the family come up with a strong consequence if the youth relapsed. They decided that the consequence would be to ostracise the son from the family for three months and to shun him if he took drugs again. The son has not gone back to drugs. [p. 86]

In this case, according to Richeport-Haley, the therapist did not need to understand the strong bond of a Latin-American family and the difficulty it has in banning a member. The goal of therapy, regardless of ethnic group, was for the family to take charge of its member and make a serious consequence rather than have the wider community do so.

In spite of this approach's apparent lack of focus on cultural and ethnic issues, paradoxically it is an approach that can be seen as more culturally congruent than other approaches that focus on these issues. As Richeport-Haley (1998) explains: (1) the family and/or social network is included in the therapy; (2) therapy does not stress exploration or insight; (3) it is action-oriented rather than discussion-oriented; (4) the therapist maintains a position of expertise and authority; and (5) the client receives concrete advice. In this approach, therapy becomes "primarily a matter of getting people to function adequately within a reality framework. The reality framework is that of eating and living and responding today, in today's realities, in preparation for tomorrow" (Erickson, quoted by Haley, 1996, p. 8). Fernando (1988) concurs with this view. Elsewhere, Fernando (1995b) also makes the following recommendations:

- for ethnic-minority clients to be listened to and heard;
- for ethnic-minority clients not to be treated as members of a homogeneous social group;

- for research to move towards undertaking process-oriented work to illuminate how structures and procedures may operate to disadvantage social groups;
- to recognize the role of power relations in research and therapeutic settings.

The eco-system approach to cross-cultural therapy takes all of these recommendations into account.

Confidentiality: a case in point

Have such cherished values as confidentiality, self-determination, autonomy, privacy, and other professional principles a place in the eco-system approach to therapy? Certainly, concepts have different meanings in cultures beyond the West. Some argue that values such as confidentiality and privacy, for example, are inconsistent with the use of family support systems and social networks (e.g. Owusu-Bempah, 1999; Silavwe, 1995). Western values may harm ethnic-minority clients because these individualist principles undermine support systems based on the family and community which provide the resources for problem-solving. This claim is supported by Hylton's (1997) study of ethnic-minority families in Britain, which demonstrated the importance of collectivist values to the well-being of ethnic-minority families.

Confidentiality in professional practice takes for granted a dichotomy between the individual and the community. It assumes that the individual is autonomous from his or her family and community. In other cultures beyond Western frontiers, however, the individual is so embedded in the community that the sense of selfhood and of psychological and spiritual sustenance is through the corporate being of one's family, group, or community. Personal problems are inevitably group problems and so are collectively resolved by the community. In traditional collectivist societies, whatever happens to the individual is also felt by the community, and vice versa. There exists a community of fate. In Western professional practice, confidentiality requires secrecy and concealment. In contrast, in collectivist cultures, "personal" problems warrant the attention and concern of one's extended family or group.

This deep sense of community should not be ignored when working with families from such backgrounds, else one might well impose an alien conception of individualism, via confidentiality, on those clients requiring much more a sense of kinship or group solidarity. For "confidentiality" to be appropriate for professional work with collectivist communities, it needs to be seen more broadly as information to be confined to, or held within, the family and community; that is, confidentiality is information or knowledge not to be shared with out-groups (Owusu-Bempah, 1999). In this context, the significance of confidentiality is its provision of safeguards for the group or community as opposed to its individual members. However, community implies a group of people with whom the client or family has close relationships, people who are interested in the client's well-being. This involves a *gemeinschaft* relationship with others rather than individuals living in close physical proximity with the client. Western values, such as confidentiality, should not be seen as invariably inappropriate for work involving ethnic-minority clients. The caution is that the application of Western principles is risky and fraught, warranting an ethic of sensitivity and caring when dealing with radically different cultures. (See Owusu-Bempah, 1999, or Silavwe, 1995, for a detailed discussion.)

Conclusion

The aim of the endeavour is to find ways of helping others more effectively. Nevertheless, in tandem with this is the possibility of a two-way process in which Western-trained practitioners not only learn to do therapy better with people of other cultures, but also learn more about their Western "selfs" in their search for personal development. Allen (1997) concludes:

> For those of us in the modern, technological, industrialized West, complex non-oppressive encounters with other concepts

of self can reveal new worlds of meaning: new ways of freeing our imaginations and of being more in touch with our emotions; of experiencing nature and the cosmos; of relating to death, time and history; of understanding and creating our own selves and our relations to others. [p. 21]

It is an excruciating process to attempt to liberate oneself from one's ethnocentric biases, especially Western ones, which have so effectively exported themselves to other parts of the world. Nonetheless, the provision of relevant services to diverse client-groups necessitates a thorough reexamination of the role of Western values and principles in all forms of counselling and therapy with ethnic minorities. This raises the need to be prepared to relinquish some of the power we wield by virtue of our professional and social status.

CHAPTER 3

Uncertainty, risk-taking, and ethics in therapy

Inga-Britt Krause

It is often observed that connecting, communicating, and being attached to others are fundamental biological processes and that human beings have developed capacities for these processes to the highest degree. Broadly, we refer to these complex human processes as social systems, society, language, or culture, and although all persons have these capacities they do not take the same shape and are not expressed in the same way everywhere. How these processes are expressed and what they mean varies according to local and specific conditions and relationships. However, at the same time as we recognize communication as a fundamental and primary process, how it is possible and can be achieved is also one of the most difficult problems for psychologists, anthropologists, physiologists, linguists, and philosophers to understand and explain. Connecting and communication is therefore an ontological problem; as such, it is not only a problem about which all cultural traditions provide a view, it is also a problem that becomes imbued with the politics of its context and changes according to prevailing power relations and ideologies. Thus, for example, capitalism as an ideology and a social system is underpinned and reinforced by rationalism, positivism, and economic theories that reduce persons to individual and autonomous "choosing machines" (Douglas & Ney, 1998), while other economies, cultural traditions, and historical contexts provide different views of individual persons and their connections with each other.

Family therapy is a mode of treatment that aims at intervening in the way persons communicate with each other, in their connections and attachments and the way these are expressed. How, then, can family therapists who work cross-culturally think about this ontological problem usefully? I think that Gellner's (1998) critique of Wittgenstein provides some useful clues about where to begin. The example is an intra-cultural one, but it applies to cross-cultural relationships and communication as well (Krause, 2001). Gellner criticizes the young Wittgenstein's statement that "death is not an event in life" (Wittgenstein, 1921, p. 72) by pointing out that

> what exactly is it that people experience when they sit on deathbeds, when they minister to the dying, or indeed are present at executions or take part in battles? What exactly is it that happens at funerals and at cremations? If death is not an event in life, just how would you describe the events in the final act of *Hamlet* or *Romeo and Juliet*? [Gellner, 1998, p. 63]

Here I do not want to pursue Gellner's further argument concerning Wittgenstein. What I want to highlight from it is that communication between persons does not depend on the parties possessing the same and identical experiences and knowledge. Indeed, there would be no reason to communicate if they did. While this is the case for intra-cultural communication, it is also generally so for cross-cultural communication, although here I must add two comments. First, it is at least theoretically possible that two persons from different cultures cannot find ways of perturbing or impressing each other. I have never heard of such a case, although I have, of course, heard of cases where one party used force or intimidation to make the other party listen or engage. Second, therefore, power, politics, and social ideologies and indeed culture always enter into communication. And this is where communication between two parties from different cultural backgrounds and of different status in a discriminatory and racist society is a special case to which family therapists must give very keen attention. In this chapter, I argue that it is precisely because communication involves uncertainty and new knowledge that cross-cultural communication is possible, but also that it is up to the therapist to ensure that such communication is respectful and non-discriminatory. This involves the therapist taking risks, and I shall give some indication of how the therapist can do this in as safe and ethical a way as may be possible.

Uncertainty

In this I am helped by one of the most significant events in the history of recent race relations in Britain. This event was the public inquiry into the death of Stephen Lawrence and the subsequent publication of an account of the inquiry in the Macpherson Report (Macpherson, 1999). The report was extremely critical of the London Metropolitan Police, and it also provided a view of discrimination that challenged earlier reports, such as the Scarman Report (Scarman, 1982), as well as the terms of earlier public debates about racism. It did this by acknowledging that discrimination and racism in public organizations such as the "Met" is institutional in the sense that there is something in the general ethos and culture of such organizations that facilitates discrimination. From an individual point of view, persons may not realize that they are doing it. It may be unwitting and thoughtless and due to collective failure and ignorance. In other words, it may be due to something that happens between persons, something in the way they collectively agree to communicate and behave. Individuals may discriminate because they are following a rule (explicitly or implicitly) or a guidance from those around them with whom they identify. Generally speaking, the latter are those persons with whom they share language and ethnicity and with whom they can agree on how things should be done and how one should think about doing it. In other words, individuals may discriminate because they are following certain cultural codes, and they may or may not be aware of this consequence of their actions and their thoughts. The observations made by Macpherson and his colleagues thus implies a view of culture as prejudicial and of prejudice as embedded in social relationships. In this they join with approaches in social psychology critical of liberal positions in which there is no theory of the production of social differences and which therefore can only explain such differences in terms of biology (Henriques, 1984). Macpherson and his colleagues put forward a radical view that challenges liberal social science as well as the politics of racism and discrimination in British society. For family therapy, it opens up opportunities.

Although it is difficult to be precise about what culture is (Krause, 1998), we can agree, that culture includes both unconscious and conscious experiences, thoughts, feelings, and behaviours. There are, then, aspects of culture that derive from our pasts, both the pasts of our parents and also our own pasts—in the sense of our infancy and what happened before we can remember. Other aspects of what we do and of our lives are not conscious to us because they are routinized and repetitive. We tend to reproduce these aspects without being aware that this is what we are doing. The aspects of our lives that are more conscious are also more within our choice. We may be more or less aware of these, and we choose to do one thing or think one thought rather than another. Although this is a simplification, this description will serve my aim here. This aim is to point out that there is both continuity and choice in culture and that it is often the continuity about which we are unaware that causes us to think that what we do and feel and think is "natural" and the only possible way that anyone can feel or do. This is where prejudice begins—not as a stance (Cecchin, Lane, & Ray, 1994), not as something bad, but as a necessary condition for communication. I am not making an excuse for those instances of discrimination that are overt, conscious, and calculated, but I am pointing out that unconscious and implicit aspects of discrimination are more difficult to address and therefore raise particular challenges. When we communicate, interact, and relate with others, we opt for one way and exclude many other possible ways. Or to put it more clearly we more-or-less opt for one way so that we can more-or-less communicate. We do not need to be exactly the same or experience exactly the same in order to communicate; it is enough that the fit is a more-or-less one, leaving some aspects a bit uncertain. Nevertheless, we always lean towards one view rather than another, otherwise communication would not be possible. We see the world through "cultural lenses" (Hoffman, 1993), particularly when the seeing is a routine of which we are unaware. In this way, continuation and choice is expressed in prejudice and uncertainty. And it is extremely important to realize that this is the same for our clients and for us. Although as mental health professionals we are trained in observing and understanding others, we also necessarily do this from our own personal and professional point of view. How, then, do we as professionals follow the lead given by Macpherson and his team?

The best place to start is to accept the prejudicial view of culture and the uncertainty that goes with it. This was recognized by John Dewey, who is said to have celebrated uncertainty as an area in which persons can experience and study practice, doing, and action, as opposed to a "spectator theory of knowledge" that emphasizes a timeless and enduring reality and order (Dewey, 1929). In this way, we may see persons not as spectators but as actors who are "actively and intelligently engaged in creating a degree of insurance despite the lack of assurance" (Whyte, 1997, p. 18). Uncertainty, then, is an aspect or an area of people's lives where something important happens and which may give valuable clues to the resilience, resources, and outlook of persons. This is also an area where family therapists and other psychotherapists aim to intervene and facilitate change for their clients. And when family therapists think and experience themselves as actors, they know this because they have uncertainty in their own lives in exactly the same way. The difficulty is that dominant professional theories lean towards the spectator view of enduring, timeless realities in which the aim is to eliminate uncertainty.

Guessing

Another way of putting this is to say that we are talking about how to understand the meaning of others and that this understanding can be "experience-near" or "experience-far" (Geertz,

1974; Kohut, 1971). Experience-far is the spectator's view, while experience-near is the actor's view. Bateson (1972) addressed this in terms of meaning and culture in an essay that is not often quoted in family therapy, "Style, Grace and Information in Primitive Art". He defined meaning in the following way:

> "Meaning" may be regarded as an approximate synonym of pattern, redundancy, information and "restraint" within a paradigm of the following sort: Any aggregate of events or objects (a sequence of phonemes, a painting, a frog, or a culture) shall be said to contain "redundancy" or "pattern" if the aggregate can be divided in any way by a "slash mark" such that an observer perceiving only what is on one side of the slash mark, can *guess*, with better than random success, what is on the other side of the slash mark. We may say that what is on one side of the slash contains *information* or has *meaning* about what is on the other side. [Bateson, 1972, pp. 103–104, emphasis in the original]

Here, Bateson points to meaning as a systemic idea. Meaning is what has gone on before, because meaning depends on the capability of others to more-or-less anticipate what will be coming next. This involves a certain amount of guesswork (Krause, 2001). Think of "Christmas", for example. It is because there has been a pattern of meaning and action and because things and symbols have been imbued with these meanings that we more-or-less know and agree on what we are talking about. Behind "Christmas" are social relations that over time have been manifest through persons acting and interacting in more or less the same ways. It has become a sort of routine, and if someone observed this and heard this being spoken about, she or he would be able to conclude not only that Christmas is a significant and meaningful cultural institution in English society, but also something about the meaning of this institution. So, from the point of view of the family therapist treating clients in therapy sessions, broadly speaking what is after the slash mark is culture. Just as Bateson (1972) placed the slash mark in his enquiry into art—"[characteristics of art object/characteristics of rest of culture]" (p. 105)—so the therapist may place "emotion"; "husband", "bride", "dress", "childcare", "respect", "nagging", and so forth on the right-hand side. In all cases we are dealing with some kind of patterning that tells us something about what is on the other side—in this case, culture or processes of interaction and communication that have some meaning for those who engage in them.

I want to make two points about this pattern. We know that it is not a reductionist one, because we know that, whatever pattern we are talking about in social systems, it must leave room for individual variation. That is to say, the pattern implicates culture without being determined by it. First, therefore, we must assume that the pattern is coherent. By this I do not mean that it must be rational, for our patients can be mistaken or deluded, just as we ourselves might be. I mean that delusions and mistakes also are culturally meaningful. Second, we cannot, a priori, know what is the meaning of the pattern. About this we can only begin by guessing in which direction we must point our questions.

> I want to illustrate this with a brief description of my work with "Alice", an 18-year-old Nigerian woman. Alice had been in care since she was 6 years old, and she had been through many unsuccessful placements with foster-carers and children's homes. Alice considered herself to be Nigerian. All her placements had been with black carers or in homes with black staff, and in some of these she had felt blamed and emotionally abused. She was referred by her social worker, who was preparing Alice for leaving the care of her present foster-mother and to begin to live independently. At this point, Alice was becoming increasingly depressed, finding it difficult to go out and generally losing her motivation for attending college and looking after herself. She was also becoming intensely preoccupied with what she called evil spirits, which she thought were inside her and which she believed her mother had sent to harm her.
>
> Alice was the second eldest of three children and had one elder sister and a younger brother. Her mother, who was also Nigerian, had been diagnosed with a mental illness and had suffered from this illness for many years, and her neglect and emotional abuse of her children had been the reason why they had all been placed in care. Alice's brother had been adopted,

while Alice and her elder sister had been placed in different children's homes. At the time when Alice came for therapy the three siblings had little contact with each other or with their mother. Their father, whom Alice described as black British and whom she could remember, had died shortly after Alice had gone into care. Alice's elder sister had been diagnosed with the same mental illness from which her mother was thought to suffer. Alice was convinced that her mother was a witch, and this together with her preoccupation with evil spirits and occasionally their voices and the presence of Alice's other symptoms had almost convinced the referring agency and the concerned social worker that Alice was suffering from an inherited mental illness. It seemed that if things became much worse, Alice would need to be admitted to an adult psychiatric ward. This was a well-meaning and concerned plan, but it was nevertheless an example of a spectator's view of Alice—that is to say, a view that did not take sufficient account of Alice's attempts to manage her own context.

When I saw Alice, I was struck by how much sense her general outlook on life made against the background of her story. She remembered her mother as a "bad mother" who did not look after her children in the past and who now also took no interest in them. She adopted a different name so as to try to protect herself from the evil spirits that her mother kept sending her way. Alice also gave the impression of being stuck and hopeless. She could not think about what needed to change or what she would want different, apart from being able to fight her mother's witchcraft more effectively. In our discussions about adolescent issues—clothes, boyfriends, girlfriends, going out, and so on—Alice emphasized the virtues of a balanced view and was not able to say much about what she herself wanted. She often said that "being unreasonable gets you nowhere" when I tried to find out about whether she was feeling angry or whether she wanted something different such as a chance to go to college, or a chance to receive some more concentrated and sustained therapeutic help than I could offer her. Alice also often asked me if I believed in evil spirits and witchcraft.

It seemed to me that there was no discontinuity between the world that Alice described and a world in which witches and bad spirits abound. Against the background of her experience she was being coherent, although suffering and unhappy. I told her this, and witchcraft and how to combat it became the frame for our conversations. We talked about witches as grabbing selfish creatures, who take what they want, maybe to revenge wrong that has been done to them. We described them as thoroughly evil and unreasonable. We also talked about how witchcraft works in those societies in which it is generally accepted that witches exist. In such societies, the power of evil may be countered by antidotes, good spirits, or good people with special powers, so that things can be set right and life can go on. Of course, there are variations in different societies, but in general there is always the possibility of balancing evil with good, injustice with justice. Since Alice's own view was very much the opposite of the evil, inconsiderate, and selfish witch, underneath the layers of the evil spirits that she thought her mother had placed upon her she was a good spirit, and much of the therapy focused on how Alice could get in touch with and extend the work of this good spirit which was in herself. Alice liked this frame; she kept coming for quite a while and made some progress. She began to go out, and she attended the entire public enquiry into the murder of Stephen Lawrence. She also eventually agreed to a referral for more intensive therapy.

There were many issues that needed addressing for Alice, and in this my work with her was just the beginning. But Alice engaged, and I think she could do this because I assumed that the way she expressed herself and what she spoke about was a coherent and meaningful response to her present predicament—namely, having had no consistent care and love and now having to face living on her own. This did not mean that I could be sure about the exact connection between what Alice had experienced and her speaking about it in terms of witches and evil spirits. My explorations with her about this had to begin with me making a guess about the sorts of questions that might be useful starting points.

Risk-taking

In my guesswork with Alice, I was taking a risk. I remember two occasions in particular that seemed to endanger my connection to Alice. The first one was when I asked whether the spirits that were interfering with her were good or bad. She answered that they were bad, in a tone that I thought suggested, "How can you ask such a stupid question? Are you sure you are on my side?" The other time was when I suggested that perhaps her mother herself was bewitched and therefore not a witch, but someone who was made to do what she did by forces bigger than herself. Alice did not like this. It was more important to her that her fears and her anger against her mother and against the world were considered to be justified. This was the frame that we both settled for, but I remember wondering whether integration in the way this is defined within a Western psychoanalytic framework (Fordham, 1974) would be a necessary step for Alice to find a path through her present difficulties and life generally. My questions about her mother could be seen to be aimed at this, but in the end I think it was my readiness to assume that Alice's worldview was coherent that enabled me to work with her and seemed to benefit her in addressing uncertainty in her daily life.

The risks I took did not come out of the blue. As I mentioned I was struck by how much sense Alice's story made to me. In this interpretation I was thinking about my own mother and how I think that she had sometimes neglected me, and I was also thinking about my daughters, one of whom is a little girl and the other is about Alice's age. I was also reminded by the ontological problem with which I began this chapter: that human beings always exist in social relationships and that the nature of these attachments have recursive influences. I remember thinking in the first session that if I were in Alice's situation, I would also feel angry and paralysed, and it was this feeling that helped me join Alice and motivated me to try to understand (Krause, 2001, chapt. 6) the meaning of what she was communicating to me. In this way, my guesswork was guided by what I knew about myself and about my own attempts to manage uncertainty. It was this self-reflection that provided me with a first pointer to how to proceed in my conversations with Alice and how to try to understand her as an actor managing her own life.

This has important implications for family therapy theory and practice, because it means that we cannot start by "not knowing", either as a true position or as a stance (Anderson & Goolishian, 1992). Indeed, such a statement does not in any way describe the state of affairs in intra-cultural or cross-cultural family therapy. A prejudicial view of culture means that we make some assumptions to the exclusion of others and that only in some instances are we aware that this is what we are doing. A "not-knowing" stance is therefore not possible. We cannot start with a clean slate even though it may often seem that this is precisely what we are doing. This is just the kind of position that at worst leads to the catalogue of failures listed in the Macpherson Report in relation to the investigation of the murder of Stephen Lawrence, and at best is likely to lead to stereotyping and inappropriate service provision for minority ethnic patient populations. Not to be aware of what we know or not to be aware that we make assumptions is perhaps our most pernicious failure. As Macpherson and his colleagues noted: the problem has to be acknowledged before it can be addressed (Macpherson, 1999, p. 31).

Ethical cross-cultural practice in family therapy

I have argued that persons do not need to be the same or to have had the same experiences in order to communicate and that it is enough that there is a more-or-less fit. It is difficult to establish a priori how much fit a more-or-less fit is; it can only be seen to be good enough in the process or in the pattern that arises through repeated processes of communication and interaction. This means that uncertainty cannot be eliminated from any kind of communication, and the greater the differences between the communicating parties, perhaps the greater the uncertainty. However, uncertainty is also an existential phenomenon experienced by all persons in all cultures and societies, because everyone has ways—which are culturally and socially constructed—that they use in order to control the course of their daily lives. In this way, we might say that uncertainty is inextricably linked to therapy, to the work of mental health professionals such as therapists and healers, to religion, and to concepts of illness and health.

If uncertainty cannot be eliminated, this also means that we take risks, although, in relation to this, one special and ubiquitous case must be mentioned: the case or cases in which power interferes. In a way, we can say that with power there are no risks, because the one who is most powerful will obviously win and the least powerful will have little choice, except perhaps to leave the field or to die. Power therefore corrupts in this case too, and communication cannot be on equal terms. But how can we be sure that power does not interfere, since power is not only something that one person has, but also something that is bestowed on persons by circumstances and by the context. Power can be as institutionalized as racism and discrimination. Even though we may not consciously aim to be outright discriminating or racist, as a group of overwhelmingly white, middle-class mental-health professionals trained in Western theories and models of the self, mental illness, malfunction, and pathology, we always in some way draw on our superior positions as professionals vis-à-vis our clients with different views. It is therefore not so easy for us to rid ourselves of the charge that we abuse our power, and it is for this reason that we must take extra steps. This is where the Macpherson Report comes to our help, because it reminds us that we must first consider our failures. We may not, in the way the policemen who were called to the site of Stephen Lawrence's murder did, assume that black people must be perpetrators of crime and cannot be victims, but we do make other assumptions in the course of our work. And as I suggested above, this cannot be otherwise. One way to start is therefore to examine our own assumptions as a starting point for better practice. This, I suggest, is what we must do in order to work with uncertainty and risk in as safe and ethical a way as may be possible, and I have suggested two steps.

The first step is to assume coherence, and this means joining in with our clients and attuning to their meanings and giving the benefit of the doubt. This does not mean that we necessarily understand, but that we benevolently assume that we will understand when we know more. The second step is to examine our own assumptions in relation to the material with which we are presented, and it is in acting on this self-reflection that we need to take risks to find out more. Traditionally, family therapists are good at this, but I am not referring to a stance, nor to the need to be seen to join with persons. We need to genuinely attempt to understand our clients and what they mean from their own point of view. And because we are different from them, we can only do this by being aware of our own. This, I think, must be a family therapist's answer to the ontological problem central to our work and to our profession.

PART III

PRACTICE PERSPECTIVES

CHAPTER 4

Ethnic sameness and difference in family and systemic therapy

Lennox K. Thomas

The question of same-culture or cross-culture practice in psychotherapy is interesting and has not seriously perplexed British-based therapists, yet it is a timely issue and needs to be debated. It is more likely that American colleagues are better acquainted with the issues because of their social and communal structures, which differ considerably from those in the United Kingdom. The question is not as simple as it first appears; the issues are, among other things, about the degree to which white therapists have an understanding of the internal and systemic effect of racism on black and ethnic-minority peoples, about the power of the majority to define the minority, as well as about the current and prevailing politics that determine the social proximity of black people to white people. If there are barriers between black and white people in our society, then the situation in therapy would reflect this. One of the problems with so-called inter-group relations is the fact that black and white are not perceived as equally different. There is a power hierarchy. The same issues about therapy and power hierarchies could be debated in relation to gender, sexuality, or disability. "Each to their own" therapy is not necessarily better, yet this therapy is the status quo in the

United Kingdom. It is the case that overwhelmingly large numbers of white therapists work with white families and individuals. This, coupled with a lack of curiosity, has led to an impoverishment of the profession of psychotherapy. The unquestioning closed loop had been the norm in therapy for a very long time until the pioneering work of family therapist Annie Lau (1984). This paper was ground-breaking work in British family therapy. While issues of culture have, for a long time, been a feature in the clinical papers by African-American writers, references to cultural issues in the British context were to do with culture and social-class structures. The work of Lau (1984), Kareem and Littlewood (1992), and Boyd-Franklin (1989) were welcome voices that annotated practice and the theories on which this depend. The interests of black and white therapists have led to some invigorating questions that are, from time to time, aired at professional conferences designed to address issues around culture and ethnicity. For sustained change to take place, these questions need to be asked in the workplace and, more importantly, at conferences that are not designed with culture or race in mind. In order for the profession to progress, we have to adopt a position that affords greater success to black, mixed, and ethnic-minority families, who are not offered therapeutic help as often as majority white families. Similarly, this group has made few demands on family and systemic therapy, but this might not remain the case for too long.

In discussing same–same or all-together therapy, we have to think about practice in both the short and long term. Choices that therapists make seem insignificant if the profession itself and its senior members do not attend to the ethical issues around complacency, discrimination, and racism in the profession. Many barriers could be removed—if not all—with the education of their members. This is an issue not only for continued professional development, but also for professional ethics. Black therapists and related workers have been concerned for many years about the value base of a hitherto white therapy and have wondered whether or not the professional precepts are not simply applied to those of a different culture with little or no modification. In minority communities, there have always been moves to develop new and appropriate ways to work with those who might not fit into the white Western framework. Some ideas have drawn on Afro-centric or other principles (Holland, 1990; Jackson, 1980). While Holland considers a social-action model with an emphasis on ethnic-minority women of a similar social group, it nevertheless has a much broader application. The view of Western orthodox therapies as value-free has lost all credibility with some practitioners and is unconvincing to others (Kareem & Littlewood, 1992; McGee & Clark, 1974). This critical position is echoed by gay men, lesbians, and people with disabilities, particularly those who espouse a social model for therapeutic intervention.

Each-to-their-own, minority therapies

Working each to their own can be most productive for groups organized around power issues in relation to the majority population. For those with therapeutic needs who also occupy a particular or relegated position in society, their needs are unlikely to be met solely by traditional or orthodox responses. Ethnicity, disability, or sexuality issues in therapy have been viewed as marginal, or at worse punitive. It is therefore not surprising that the process of each-to-their-own therapy extends to the function of self-validation for some and to the process of dismantling the inferior identity that is often given to the foreigner, the outsider, or the social minority. From this point of view, each-to-their-own therapy serves a useful purpose. It is not surprising that the minorities in therapy often examine their social position in relation to the majority. This seems a useful way of contextualizing whatever psychological or family problems that they might have. It would seem equally helpful to social-majority people in therapy to consider their relation to minority groups, yet this is unlikely to happen until therapists are brave enough to face these questions in their own training and preparation for practice.

When this eventually happens, majority therapists will be able to facilitate majority patients and clients in considering the validity of their superior "ready-made identities" in relation to social minorities. There are both economic and social rewards for a society that marginalizes or excludes minority people. In this supreme position, it is acceptable/preferable to be able-bodied, white, and non-gay, so it seems that nothing is gained by giving up this advantage and the opportunities it provides. On the face of it, there are only losses; however, the real gains are those of fair play and personal integrity. The belief in entitlement and being in the rightful place at the front of the line prevents many white people from seeing themselves as they really are. For the profession to really work effectively for black and ethnic minorities, therapists also have to work effectively with white-majority people. Therapeutic effort has to go into dismantling the false sense of themselves that white people have historically been raised to have. This is an endeavour that will not be readily undertaken. Black and ethnic people are not new to the painful task of self-appraisal—this has been a process that has taken many years, from the point of colonization to the arrival in the land of the colonizer. Young black people have to deal with self-appraisal and self-esteem issues overtly and subliminally on a daily basis. Until this taking stock is done by us all in our society, working all together in a melting-pot fashion will always exact a higher price for the black or minority client and the black or minority therapist.

Each-to-their-own minorities working together therapeutically could be of great benefit, though this might not always be the case. Working in this way makes it possible for those who share a particularly oppressed position to have a better understanding of how the external struggles have impacted on family systems and on their internal psychological structures. Public humiliation of refugee and asylum-seeking families will no doubt erode confidence and create a sense of shame in them. Those seeking help are likely to experience an easier joining with the therapist even if this does not guarantee a smooth run later on in the therapy. Black therapists have to be alert to the effects of internalized racism on clients (Thomas, 1992, 1995b) and how this might affect joining. The obvious benefit of same–same therapy for those in minority groups is the fact that to some extent the therapist will have some experiences (if not all) that mirror those of the patient. Working each to their own in this context could help clients who have culturally appropriate ways of understanding and dealing with an issue that might seem not only alien to majority therapists but pathological or dysfunctional. The therapist from a similar background will not only be more able to give greater consideration and meaning to the matter, but will also be better equipped to make an intervention. The scope and range of the intervention will give greater authenticity to the therapeutic work. In this context, the therapist will be making greater use of him/herself, probably overtly in the sessions to help clients understand situations that they both might share, but certainly to reflect quietly on those matters that they have experienced personally. Thomas (1992, 1995b) discusses the effect on the black therapist of witnessing the pains of self-discovery in patients that they themselves have experienced, and how this can lead either to a greater empathy or to a distancing of oneself from the painful reminder.

It is perhaps inescapable that minorities in a dominant majority society will to varying degrees internalize distorted or negative views of themselves, particularly if they have ingested stereotyped images and views that have been generated in order to support majority belief in their own superiority. These negative and self-loathing views have to be worked through in a safe and trusting space so that restructuring can take place in therapy with families and individuals. Being an outsider or being on the margins of society affects many aspects of the social world of those we seek to help as much as it does the helpers. To have as a reference point someone from one's own minority community can perform more than a clinical function. For young and aspiring black and minority clients, seeing the image of themselves in a position of trust as a professional can serve to boost self-esteem and help them to visualize themselves as also being able to perform a useful role in society. This added value of black and minority therapists working with their own can go a long way towards helping clients to shake off negative views of themselves accrued over many years.

Each-to-their-own therapy can have as many potential difficulties as benefits. As mentioned briefly earlier, internalized racism can have an insidious effect on relationships between black people. I am not sure of the extent to which among other minority groups similar mechanisms exist that serve to distance the one from the other. The oppression of minorities in society often leads to them in turn oppressing themselves. As members of society, minorities learn the ways and means of their own downfall, thus, acerbic humour, put-downs, and insults can never cut as deeply as those generated in their own community about those within it.

Therapy with one's own can at times be an arena where battles for hierarchy of ideas or personhood are contested. Great care has to be exercised so that unspoken envy or intolerance of difference does not wreck what seemed like a therapeutic haven. The games that are played out among minority groups in society are equally around supremacy or hierarchy. Until some fifty years ago, among the colonized people of the Caribbean those members of the community with lighter skin tones, who in some way resembled the European masters, were at the top of the ladder of social esteem. In recent years, this belief has been in some ways inverted. Now, esteem is conferred on those who espouse an African value and cultural base, sometimes with the visible trappings of their African heritage.

The Africanization of Caribbean and American black people has been a progressive and positive trend since the dawn of the twentieth century. The yearning to return to Africa was never quenched, and there were several movements in the English-speaking Caribbean and the United States alone, both Bedward and the Niabingies in Jamaica and the Black Star Line conceived by Marcus Garvey. The followers of the Honourable Elija Mohamed sought to make their home in the United States through their vision of a self-sufficient black Muslim community. Many of these movements came in the wake of early work and writings by W. E. B. Du Bois (1906). These positive moves to discard the degraded identities ascribed to black people can, sadly, also be used as a badge of superiority over their own. How this gets played out in social situations is reflected in the therapeutic setting. Similarly, these intra-group politics take place in other types of minority therapies. Who is the most radical Out-Gay man, Lesbian, or Feminist is also an issue to be dealt with in minority each-to-their-own therapy. If taken seriously, however, a great contribution can be made by minority therapies to the body of systemic and psychodynamic theories. The very fact that they are minority therapies will make it difficult for majority therapists to feel able to learn from them. It would, after all, defy all logic that any other than majority-group therapists could contribute anything of worth. It might help to undermine the thinking that helps to keep in place the view that each-to-their-own minority therapy might not be real therapy, but an indescribable something else.

Working each to their own is a challenge in minority communities, but the most exercised are those who might have to supervise clinical work while not fully understanding the mechanisms and manoeuvres that are taking place simply because supervisors do not belong to the same or any other minority culture.

How black and minority staff get supported in same–same therapy: a cause for concern

Working as a therapist in the late 1970s, many of the cases involving black individuals and families were given to me. Some came from colleagues who felt stuck and thought that I might be able to get somewhere with them. While I had my own full complement of cases, the majority of them being white, my white colleagues were approaching me in the corridors and on the stairs and asking me to rescue them by taking over their black clients. At the same time, it was said in the team that they did not want to see me carrying all the black cases; however, this situation of working with most of the black clients came about by the team surreptitiously decanting their cases onto me. I felt too new, on the one hand, to challenge it; on the other hand, I was happy, in conjunction with one other white colleague, to work with a majority of black clients. My ability to question what was going on did not emerge until a colleague I passed in the corridor said in jest, "I hope that you are not plotting with all those black families that you are seeing." After the humour wore off, I wondered what on earth he meant by that and felt that I was being accused of something. I realized that there was some guarded hostility in the team towards me for, on the face of it, having the ability and therefore the power to spare them the exposure of working with black cases about which they had doubts and, at the same time, showing them up for their deficiencies.

Consistent, of course, with the history between blacks and whites in the Americas and the Caribbean, black people were viewed as a threat if they were seen to be getting on well together. The rule of the plantation was that the black slaves were to be kept apart and metaphorically speaking, at each other's throats. Keeping them antagonistic towards each other required a judicious mixing of the disparate African tribal groups, relying on one favourite tribal group or mulattos to dominate the others and keep them in line and who, in turn, were hated by all the others. By this skilful manipulation, the white masters were protected. Cooperation among the Africans was the last thing that was wanted. It is therefore not surprising that black therapists and black patients and clients working successfully together will arouse suspicion in some white professionals. Similar difficulties arise in staff groups when black workers choose to meet together for support and to discuss issues of mutual concern. The fact that most professional meetings are white caucus groups seems to cause little concern. If indeed same–same minority therapy is to develop beyond the simple fact of similar or same ethnicity, a great deal of meeting, talking, and theory-building has to take place between black therapists. Each-to-their-own practice has to be underpinned by the ideas and precepts that are valued and sustained in the same communities. Some of the arguments are debated in Jackson (1980) and McGee and Clark (1974). While this position would be generally true, there should also be some space for challenge without a convergence of views and identities. There also needs to be scope to allow for difference, for not all African-descended people share the same views. Those who share minority-group communities are as different and as varied as majority white people. When black and other ethnic-minority people cease worrying about their collective identity, they can also claim their social class, political, gender, disability, and sexuality difference and also be black. Introducing ideas about minority therapies into the mainstream has proved to be an uphill struggle. However, the slowly increasing numbers of black therapists makes it more likely that papers and research will, in time, appear on working with black families and individuals.

Papers such as those of Jackson (1980) and McGee and Clark (1974) will help to chart new ideas for working with black families and make a lasting impression. New and useful ways of working will be able to present the unique connection between therapists' and clients' cultural backgrounds. If details of minority therapies are not disseminated, the innovative ways in which culture is used will not be discussed sufficiently in order to discover what is potentially useful and what is not.

The K Family

In the wake of a child-abuse disclosure, a mother of Caribbean descent was left by her husband to cope with its grim after-effects. The 13-year-old daughter talked of the cumulative sexual abuse at school. Her 9-year-old sister had not been abused. The relationship between the mother and the older daughter was under some strain, and the girl took to staying out at nights with local trouble-makers and getting into trouble at school. The stress on Mrs K proved too much and she was admitted to hospital after a breakdown. After a quick but good recovery, both mother and daughter attended separate groups for families after abuse, but neither found this helpful. Mrs K referred herself and her daughters to a community psychotherapy service for family therapy. The referral was argued about at a team meeting, and Dr A, a female Middle-Eastern therapist, began the work but was given notice of an imminent admission to hospital with a month's post-operative recovery. Reluctantly, after three weeks the family was passed to me as her successor. In my view, Dr A was the ablest person to work with this family, and I was reluctant to work with abused girls and their mothers and rarely undertook this work. I agreed to take the referral because I had an alliance with Dr A, who worked in a way similarly to myself, and she would not have been happy with plans to offer mother and daughter individual long-term therapy, as the team had in mind.

At our first session, mother and older daughter did not talk; they could barely tolerate being together in the same room, and the younger sister was their go-between. The younger daughter spoke for both of them and spoke easily to them both. I set the non-communicating pair a variety of tasks and recruited the younger daughter as a member of the observing/supervising team. Having been excluded from school, the older girl was around the home from time to time with her mother, but in separate rooms. I began by getting them to sit together on the sofa in my consulting-room, then to hold hands, and I then asked them to do this at home while viewing television. I would from time to time check with the younger daughter on progress. She would report that things were going very well and that her mother and sister were carrying out the tasks. Mrs K requested that in future I had phone contact with the younger child, whom she wanted to be settled in school and would therefore not be attending sessions. As the weeks progressed, the mother-and-daughter pair would come to therapy having been on shopping trips or days out sightseeing. I then changed the task to mutual hair brushing and braiding. After initial reluctance because, she said, she did not understand why they had to do this, Mrs K eventually enjoyed the task with her daughter. They were happy that they were once again connected, and her daughter was no longer staying out at nights away from home. They were planning for the older girl to return to school and for the mother to go on computer skills courses.

Mrs K had been most reluctant at first to carry out the attachment exercises, but she was very happy with the outcome. She told me that she probably should be coming to therapy with her own mother, whom she could never get on with. This therapeutic intervention was very culturally specific and relied on the therapist's experience of witnessing proximity and attachment between Caribbean and African mothers and daughters. Hair brushing, combing, and braiding are very important, not just for grooming but also for bonding. Hawkes (1995), a psychoanalytic psychotherapist, sees haircare in African-Caribbean communities as having great social significance during the early years of migration. While it was clear to see what had gone on between mother and daughter, little hypothesizing needed to take place. It is my view that prescribing solutions for their problems was made easier because of my closeness to their culture. I knew from my commonplace, everyday experience of the significance of African mother–daughter haircare and its importance as attachment behaviour. Mrs K found in this the answer to her problem of not being able to talk to her daughter. There had been no doubt in my mind that there had at some stage been a very loving relationship between the two, and I saw it as my task to rekindle that love so that whatever natural healing was available in this family could take place. As she saw it, what I required of them seemed too ordinary and had nothing to do with what they had come for. I managed to encourage her gently, with some degree of authenticity, that they needed to try it out. It seemed that the very ordinariness of day-to-day physical contact and the significance of it could mend a breach where words could not.

Each-to-their-own, majority therapies

When those from majority cultures work together in same-same therapies, the process is little examined in terms of power, identity, or culture or in relation to minority cultures. Minority therapies inescapably have to address these issues of context because they have a powerful and controlling effect on their lives and contribute to the formation of their identity. Being white in white-majority cultures—and sometimes in white-minority cultures—often confers on one certain unquestioned privileges. The opportunity to examine issues of this particular privilege does not often seem to present itself in white-majority therapies. It seems that the social privilege and power of men in relation to women in society is not often explored in men's therapy. Power-holders do not use therapy to examine the power that they possess, how this might be in direct relation to those who possess less power, and how significant this might be in the acquiring of their identity. The white therapist and white client is what is often written about; this is the regular situation, what is known, and what is the gold standard in both individual and family therapy. Identity issues around whiteness and its relation to blackness or brownness is a non-issue, and only by chance might it get triggered in therapy and thereby provide a challenge to both white patient and white therapist.

As a supervisor of a white male therapist treating a white British-born man of Mediterranean extraction, I was taken aback by the patient's virulent racist comments. He came to therapy with a severe grief reaction after the death of his sister, who had been a drug user over a long period of time. They had been in care from a young age, and he felt a sense of responsibility as the older sibling. They both dabbled with drugs in a mixed group of friends while in care, but he had managed to adopt a more stable lifestyle. He achieved a reasonable amount of success as a family man and a small-businessman. He blamed the blacks for introducing his sister to drugs, although he had first described the group of friends as mixed. He also did not consider why it was that he gave up his drug use but his sister did not. In fits of rage, the patient talked about killing all the scum, blacks, gays, foreigners. My supervisee found it difficult to talk about this man's racism and homophobia, though he unconvincingly stated that he did not find working with him a problem. I was surprised at this because I had learned almost a year after working with the supervisee that his wife was a black Caribbean woman. I wanted to know what he thought the patient required of him after these outbursts, and what was going on for him, as the therapist, when these things get said. He said that he was frightened at what this man might say or do next. He even feared at times that the patient has the potential to be a serial killer. He did at times wonder whether he was being taunted as a woolly liberal type and at other times whether the patient wanted him to join in or agree with his verbal tirades. Tempted on one occasion to tell the patient that his wife was black, he resisted it, feeling that his marriage to a black woman could not be used as a mark of his decent liberal outlook, nor could he do this in order to be rid of the patient. After some time, he was able to engage in a more questioning stance to the patient and allowed himself to be more honest about the patient and the feelings evoked in him by the bigoted material.

Each-to-their-own majority therapy can at times seem restricted, insular, and self-contained. In this particular situation, the patient assumed the therapist to be the same as himself. While they were both white men, the contexts of their lives were poles apart. The means of escaping from the circularity of sameness to contemplate issues of hierarchy, power, or difference or even the assumption of sameness in majority therapies has very creative potential. The majority therapist can offer the patients the opportunity to work on their issues in relation to minority groups, and this in turn will lead to a truer identity in relation to self and others.

Some majority white people feel very identified with black and minority people for many reasons, and exploration of this would be useful. It would appear to be the case that few majority white clients would choose to explore issues around a falsely acquired superior identity. This belief in white supremacy has existed for many years among white communities and therefore runs particularly deep. In all white communities, the rule of law supported this belief and myths were generated to perpetuate the notion of black inferiority and white superiority. It is my view that therapeutic work is incomplete if these matters go unaddressed in contemporary society. The sad fact is that this will not happen in each-to-their-own majority therapy until senior therapists are able to do the same exploration. The professional structures are flawed because those highly esteemed in the psychotherapy profession are likely to be as personally ill equipped to deal with issues of context as are its patients and most recent recruits. Until this change process takes place, black clients will feel unprotected and vulnerable in relation to majority therapists' views about race and other minority issues. Similarly, black therapists might not have the confidence of knowing that their white co-therapist will be able to deal with what black and white patients might bring to the therapy in regards to race. Black co-workers are too often seen as midwives who will deliver white colleagues from difficult race situations, yet they do not receive a commensurate level of support.

Kofi

"Kofi", a black male therapist, brings an issue of concern to an informally set up black support group. He said that he had worked with a white female therapist in his team at a family centre for some three years. On a recent visit to a local health centre to attend a pre-conference meeting, Kofi felt uneasy about what was said as an aside during the discussion of the black family that they are working with. A member of the health team felt able to say that most of the young black mothers failed to keep clinic appointments for their under-fives. This comment had no apparent relevance to the discussion of the case. As the only black person in the room, he was silenced in shock wondering why this was said. No one responded to the comment, and after the meeting his co-therapist apologized for not saying anything. He said that he felt betrayed, because he supported her in debates about practice and gender in the team.

Surprised that this had happened, he wondered why it was such a challenge for white majority people to have discourses about oppressive behaviour and language without input from black people. From the discussion that followed, others in the support group said that the net effect was that black workers tend to avoid situations where they might be vulnerable. For Kofi, the failure of his colleague to support him served as a litmus test of their working relationship and personal friendship.

Working in an each-to-their-own manner, majority therapy has a long way to go in terms of helping majority white people to acquire the knowledge to understand their place in the wider social context and acquire the skills to live, work, and interact with those in minority communities. In relation to this, the therapeutic process needs to help those with an inflated sense of their importance in relation to our total world family.

Cross-cultural practice

Cross-cultural practice recognizes that people are raised in ways that might prevent them connecting with each other at a social or emotional level. Having recognized this fact, therapists can find sensitive ways to make connections and learn about both themselves and others. One of the guiding principles is that we should not think of our ways of doing things as normal but as different and that we stand just like other cultures—no better, no more normal, than any other. As a means of preparing to work all together, issues of context, power, and supremacy have to be addressed. Once this has been attended to, there is no reason why people of different cultures and backgrounds cannot work effectively together. This simple baseline for therapeutic practice is a challenge to the psychotherapies. Cross-cultural therapy (Kareem & Littlewood, 1992) is interested in the impact of cultural and social power on relationships and how this gets represented both inside and outside the therapy. Here even same–same therapy has the potential of being an intercultural therapy, since same ethnicity contact can have in it finely tuned differences of social class, disability, sexuality, and gender. Most therapies have some element of working across a cultural boundary because of personal and familial difference. Respecting difference and being interested in the context of the family and their journey to where they are is often a good respectful way to start. Extensive knowledge of the other person's culture is not necessary, and therapy should work well as long as the therapist is open to knowing and learning about their own culture and its impact on themselves in this new situation. Effective therapeutic work is being done when the therapist does not rigidly hold on to his or her view of the world as the only one but has an awareness of many potential others. By its very nature, cross-cultural or intercultural therapy relies on mixed teams to be most effective. Good team-work in a clinical setting, explored in Cooklin (1999), relies on the exploration of difference and valuing diversity. Each team member brings a difference that becomes a component part of the whole.

Change is difficult in teams that do not maintain the same line up from decade to decade but from time to time introduce a new team member whose views match their own thereby preserving professional opinion, presenting no challenge, and effecting no change. We as therapists expect to see change in the families and individuals we work with, yet it is something we ourselves frequently resist in the workplace. Working with family systems often relies on background from our own families or substitute families. Knowingly or otherwise, we reach into our own experiences and bring this to bear on our work with client families. What we tap into might not always be helpful; however, it is often an indication of where we are in our own puzzles with families and our place in or outside them. It is particularly helpful in mixed teams doing cross-cultural family therapy to spend some time usefully doing genogram work together (Lieberman, 1979). While this might have been part of the qualifying training, the process of doing a family genogram in culturally mixed teams helps to contextualize some aspects of cultural values and beliefs. Because of the reliance on team members, family work demands genograms as a team exercise. Cross-cultural work with families has to extend beyond the differences that exist between all families to consider the differences and influences of religion and ethnicity, with the subtle meanings they might have for family life. If active team training is not undertaken (Miller & Thomas, 1994; O'Brian, 1990), the problems that families present will, like a barium meal, show up the flaws in the team system.

Sue and Tim

"Sue", a black woman, has worked with "Tim", a white man, for almost two years in a child and family consultation service. They have worked with other colleagues on cases in the past, but in recent months they have talked about writing something for a professional journal. They have just started working with "Meg", a white woman aged 35, and her family. The family were referred because Meg had difficulties caring for her three youngest children, aged 2, 4,. and 8 years, and "Marley", her 14-year-old son, who was referred for truanting from school. Her eldest, "Dawne", is doing very well at school and at home. Having fractured a bone in her ankle and been admitted to hospital at the age of 8 years, it has been Dawne's ambition to be a nurse on a children's ward. Meg had a serious drink and drugs problem in the past but would describe herself now as a social drinker. She gave up a heroin substitute in rehabilitation before the birth of "Mimi", her youngest, now 2 years old. All of the children—Dawne, Marley, "Petra", "Luke", and "Miriam" (Mimi)—attend the sessions. Meg is trying to get her life together after many years of substance misuse.

Meg met "Peter", the father of her two older children, at school, where they were in the same class. Peter is locally born of Caribbean descent. Petra and Luke have the same white father, "Trevor", who is actively around in their lives; Mimi was a bit of a surprise pregnancy. She was conceived when Meg was at her lowest, and the father is apparently white and unknown. Meg jokes that he could be one of many men. Meg explained that Peter is the love of her life even though he is now married to someone else. He left her when Marley was 4 years old and has been antagonistic towards her ever since. He discovered that his best friend, Trevor, was supplying her with drugs and that she repaid him with occasional sex. Trevor, she says, has always been good to her and the children. Although he is the father of Petra and Luke, she has never ever really loved him. Trevor lives in the next road and helps out with the children on a daily basis. Meg admits that when he is not around, the care of the younger ones falls to Dawne and Marley, who are adored by them. Trevor gave up drugs, drink, and sex three years ago and lives a reformed life dedicated to Buddhism, which he feels saved his life. Although he wanted to be part of the family meetings, Meg refused, saying that family are only those who live under her roof. Asked by Tim if Peter might like to be part of the meetings, Meg replied that Pete was an idiot like most of the black men she has had contact with. She added that even now, after all these years, he refuses to talk to Trevor. Both therapists notice Marley's unease, and in discussing the session later that day Sue wondered whether or not Meg's views might cause upset to the children, particularly Dawne and Marley. Both Sue and Tim thought that this issue should be raised the next time.

The session came and went, but the matter was not raised. At the end of that session, Tim said that he thought Sue was going to discuss the issue because she was so at ease with the material, and particularly as she is married to a white man. He added that the team had learned so much since she gently prodded them into taking on some of these issues of race and difference. At this point Sue—who is usually calm—explodes, telling him that it was high time that the team stopped looking to her to take all the risks and that he himself will have to raise those issues that concern him. She said that she was not good at dealing with race issues in therapy, that she was a family therapist who dealt with all the issues that are presented and so should he. She said that he would see it as her expertise, because for too long it was left to her and she did not have the luxury of ignoring it. The incident was discussed at a team meeting, and Sue told her colleagues that they will have to start thinking about ways to deal with race issues in the clinical work because her feelings of betrayal about the way they have treated her is taking a toll on her husband, with whom she discusses these matters. She told them that she has to reach deep into her personal resources to deal with team issues of race but has noticed too many team members simply sidestepping the whole matter. Her colleagues expressed surprise at what Sue had said, but they agreed that she did have a point. They also reaffirmed the view that having all team members contribute to an understanding of intercultural work is to allow more than one cultural perspective to be brought to bear on an issue. For example, the way that Tim experienced working with the family might be different to how Sue felt—Tim being male and white, Sue female and black. While Tim felt sensitive to Marley's feelings, he probably also felt pushed out and insignificant just as Trevor might have felt excluded by Meg. It was important for Tim to talk to his co-therapist about what was going on for him in the clinical work. However, he formulated the remedy by himself, expecting his colleague to undertake it and thereby excluding himself from what he thought was the difficult part.

The team persuaded the two of them to stick it out with the work and gave them some ideas to pursue in order to move things on. Tim was to raise more than what the team saw as the ubiquitous "race issues". He was to get alongside Marley to ask about how males were treated in the family. Marley responded to Tim, saying that he did not like the way that his mother treated Trevor. He said that she was always calling him horrible names and always said that men were bastards, especially his dad, whom he will just grow up to be like. The space was helpful for Marley, who was able to talk about what he felt was hurtful to him. Like the team's surprise on learning of Sue's feelings, Meg was able to hear—for the first time, it seemed—what her son was feeling. After a little encouragement on claiming that she was not a huggy type of person, Meg was able to show him some warmth and tenderness for his hurt. All the children wanted Trevor to attend family meetings, and Meg reluctantly agreed. As a significant carer, Trevor took his place in the therapy. Tim also took his place as a therapist and no longer as a bystander to the important events that were taking place in the therapy. Once Meg and the family were in a position to consider how Marley felt, they had the opportunity to think about some of the racially abusive things that affected them all as a family.

Good mixed team-work will take place after both team and personal development. Without this factor, teams will continue to operate at the level of colonizing black and minority therapists who join them. To resist this, minority therapists need to be aware of the skills that they bring and the particular vantage points that they have on therapy practice. Minority therapists bring their experience of living both in their cultural context and in that of the wider framework of the society as a whole. The experience of having developed a synthesis of these cultures will inevitably enable them to bring useful skills to psychotherapy. Intercultural or all-together therapy enables practitioners to push out the frontiers of therapeutic skill and understanding.

Conclusion

At a time of social unrest and movement, when in order to flee communal violence groups of people are seeking refuge in far-off countries, the issues of working cross-culturally or in our communities will become all the more pressing and important. The United Kingdom, unlike some western European countries, has favoured generalist services probably because the migrants to the United Kingdom in the past have in the main been from Commonwealth countries, with some history of the English language and culture (Thomas, 2000). With new migration and asylum seeking, this is no longer the case. Being in therapy with someone whose culture and background is similar to one's own will have therapeutic benefit. This will work particularly well when the therapist is skilled enough to recognize when and if the therapy is retreating too far into the comfort of sameness to avoid difference and change. Avoiding the challenge of difference and change is a potential pitfall when client and therapist share cultures, and particularly so when they are both from power-holding sections of majority cultures. Two people in minority cultures working together can similarly be caught up in an insular therapy unless the therapist has the capacity to look beyond the confines of his or her own community. Cross-cultural therapeutic work does not only present a learning opportunity but very personal challenges to beliefs and stereotypes. Both modes of therapeutic practice can be adopted in the same teams, since both have something to offer families and individuals.

CHAPTER 5

The African Families Project: a black and white issue

Amma Anane-Agyei, Wendy Lobatto, & Philip Messent

Beginnings

When black families in the United Kingdom come into contact with "helping" agencies such as social services departments and child and adolescent mental health services, these encounters often do not go well. Black families are more likely than white families to receive "hard-end" interventions from such agencies, with their children being placed on the child-protection register, made the subject of a care order, or receiving serious diagnoses. Barn et al. (1997) found that more black children were the subject of child-protection investigations. Other studies (Rowe et al., 1989; MacDonald, 1992; Barn, 1993) demonstrate the overrepresentation of black children in the public care system and a lack of appropriate preventative support services. It is not surprising that black parents are suspicious about such agencies, seeing social workers as making negative judgements about their ways of parenting their children and mental health services as stigmatizing. Such agencies are seen as representing the majority white culture and hence lacking understanding of black families' values and ways of raising children.

Fatimilehin and Coleman (1998) quoted one African-Caribbean parent talking about this perceived gap in understanding:

> "You don't know where he is coming from, he doesn't know where you're coming from, you know what I mean? And you're talking and you don't know if they're understanding you.... So there would be no trust, there's nothing there to begin with, there's not a foundation to build on." [p. 9]

Social workers and other professionals coming into contact with black families will tend to interpret such wariness as evidence of an unwillingness to cooperate and will feel justified in making the negative judgements that such families are fearing, leading to a vicious cycle in which both parties to the interaction feel that their negative beliefs about the other party are increasingly borne out.

The African Families Project sprung from an observation of this very unhealthy dynamic, which it seemed was particularly likely to occur with families from Africa who were relatively recent arrivals in the United Kingdom and hence were less familiar with local institutions and customs than were earlier migrant groups. (The project takes as its target group families where children or their parents have been born in Africa.) One member of the initial project team [A.A.-A.], herself of African origin, was a social worker based in a specialist child-protection team and involved on a daily basis in working with African families subject to such negative judgements by other professionals. The others [P.M., W.L.], both of white British origins, were social workers based within the local multidisciplinary child and adolescent mental health service (CAMHS). African children only seemed to be referred successfully to the service when they had particularly severe symptoms, requiring urgent psychiatric assessment (Messent & Murrell, forthcoming). African children and young people with less serious problems were not referred or tended not to engage with the service offered when they were referred. Self-referrals were rare.

The project began then with joint working between these workers based in these different contexts. African families coming to the attention of the child-protection social-work team, where there were child mental health concerns, would be referred to the CAMHS and a piece of joint work would ensue, addressing both child-protection and child mental health issues. Similarly, African families referred to CAMHS where there were some child-protection concerns would be referred to the child-protection team in order to initiate a collaborative piece of work, aimed at addressing both sets of issues. Since these tentative beginnings, the project team has expanded to include other health professionals within CAMHS, social workers from assessment and family support teams, and a counsellor based in a local health centre.

The project team has also attempted to maintain a balance between black workers with origins in different parts of Africa and white workers, so that in each co-working partnership both traditions, both ways of seeing, could be represented.

Working principles

Engagement

It was assumed by members of the project team that parents referred would bring with them a feeling of mistrust and apprehension. Where child-protection concerns have been raised by other professionals, such parents will feel that they are being judged negatively and will tend to see all agencies as joining in such a view of them. Hence the first working principle evolved by the project team was that *in making an initial connection with such families, every effort should be made to communicate a respect for parents' good intentions*—their wish to raise their children to be successful members of the community. In follow-up interviews with parents conducted by independent workers after the termination of contact, they often referred to this appreciation by project workers of their underlying concern for their children, as compared to other agencies which were seen as judging them negatively.

> "The fact that I have a loud voice with my children doesn't mean that I don't love them. . . . Wendy understood that my way of speaking to the children was loving."

This principle of respect for parents' good intentions did not include minimizing in any way the seriousness of child-protection concerns. *Where child-rearing methods out of keeping with societal standards had been used such as physical chastisement, parents would be given information about how such methods were viewed and what the consequences would probably be if they were persevered with.* The rights and responsibilities of social workers to ensure that children are adequately protected under the terms of the Childrens Act would be explained, as well as the likely consequences of parents being seen as non-cooperative. Such information would be presented in a manner that communicated an underlying respect for them as fundamentally caring parents who were in need of this information in order not to be misunderstood by professionals with whom they were coming into contact.

One of the ways in which workers would communicate respect for parents would be *always beginning contact with a meeting in which the nature of any work to be undertaken would be discussed without the children present*. This avoided the possibility of parents' position of authority in the family being undermined in front of their children, and it left them with the power to decide about their involvement in any ongoing work.

> The G family were referred to the child-protection team, and the son's name ("John", aged 10 years) placed on the child-protection register after it had become apparent that he was regularly being locked in the bathroom by his parents as a punishment. It was explained to them by A.A.-A. how such actions were viewed, and alternative methods of "getting through to" John were suggested. John was also presenting behavioural problems at his school and was bed-wetting; a referral to the African Family Project was therefore proposed so that these difficulties could be addressed. The parents initially then met with A.A.-A. and P.M. without the children present, so that the nature and extent of any ongoing work could be explained, without undermining the parents' authority in the family. It was agreed that they would bring their children along to a subsequent meeting, and that the focus of the work would be helping John with his bed-wetting problem

and helping him establish a new sort of reputation at his school (his parents felt that John had already improved there, but that changes were not being recognized).

This initial focus embodies a further organizing principle: *that the focus of our work should always be specific and comprehensible,* making the anticipated outcome the success of the young person and the ending of the involvement of the social services department. Boyd-Franklin (1989) has similarly emphasized the importance of making goals explicit and concrete when engaging with black families in the United States. Furthermore, the anticipated number of appointments and duration of the contact are spelt out, recognizing the family's other commitments and organizing sessions as much as possible to fit in with those commitments. Many of the African parents the project has worked with have complex and demanding work schedules, involving shifts and antisocial hours. The impact of work commitments on attendance at follow-up appointments would also be recognized, with letters and phone calls routinely being used to remind them of forthcoming appointments.

Working with children and young people: re-establishing connections

Many of the families referred to the project had histories of dislocation. Some families had been fractured by civil war, with parents separated for several years from their children and neither party having any contact or news of the other's well-being. Other families had been separated during the process of migration, with some children having been left behind for several years with extended-family members in Africa while parents established themselves in the United Kingdom. Once reunited the process of assimilation into a cohesive family unit was problematic for many of these families. Project workers used an "eco-map" as a standard measure of children and young people's integration into their family unit early in their work, getting each individual child to map out their interrelationships in order of closeness and importance.

John G and his sister "Mary" had spent six years with an aunt in Ghana before being re-united with their parents a year before their referral to the project. Both siblings placed both parents as relatively insignificant in their eco-map, rating as more important (in John's case) a neighbour's dog and his Sega Megadrive.

This disconnectedness is viewed by project workers as particularly significant in African families, for whom identity has traditionally been collective rather than individual, as expressed in the African proverb:

"I am because we are, and because we are, therefore I am."
[Mbti, 1969, p. 141]

One of the aims of the work is therefore *to re-establish connections between child and family, and sometimes with the wider community, in order that such a collective identification can become more of a realistic possibility.* In the case of John and his sister, the implications of their eco-maps were discussed with their parents, and mechanisms established within the family to ensure that there were more positive interactions between the children and both parents. Mr and Mrs G understood the importance of making sure that their children felt in closer communication with them, making opportunities within their busy daily schedule for talking with the children. One measure of the success of this piece of work were the eco-maps John and Mary completed at its termination, nine months later, in which relationships with their parents, siblings, and extended family had become the most important and significant in their lives.

Eco-maps have proven a more appropriate tool for use with African families than the genogram, which is more often utilized as a way of gathering information about family relationships. Watts-Jones (1997) has similarly argued that genograms are inadequate for African-American families because of the underlying assumption with a genogram that "family" is strictly a biological entity, as opposed to a kinship based on both biological and functional ties.

With some other children and young people, the process of re-connection is much more problematic. Adolescents in particular may find an identification with peer-group interests and values as compelling, and a longer period of individual work may be necessary to find meaningful ways of establishing links with their family and wider community. The presence of African workers on the project team is particularly essential during this sort of work, in that they are able to invite young people to join them in a sense of connection with this wider culture. They also act as a powerful role model, demonstrating the possibility of maintaining a positive African identity while also establishing a successful career (counterbalancing, in some measure, the negative images of Africa presented in the media).

Working with families to re-establish "safe" parental authority

Parents coming into contact with the child-protection system will frequently feel resentful and dis-empowered, judged as failing by a group of professionals from a different class and culture (MacKinnon, 1998). As mentioned above, one important method used by project members in establishing an initial connection with African parents is to demonstrate an appreciation of their good intentions—that the parents have their children's interests at heart. Another important method of giving a feeling of power and control back to parents, also mentioned above, is to give them clear information about where they stand in relation to the interventions of statutory organizations like social services departments: information about the Childrens Act, the rights and duties it places on local authorities, the workings of the child-protection system, and the steps necessary to conclude the involvement of such agencies with their families. It is necessary to present such information in an atmosphere of calm, and over a considerable period of time, giving parents plenty of opportunity to come back with questions and concerns. The extreme level of anxiety generated in some African families when coming into contact with statutory agencies was exemplified by one project referral where a mother had been charged with an assault carried out upon a policeman who had visited her household in order to investigate child-protection concerns about her teenage daughter.

Parents in families who are being told that the methods of maintaining parental authority that they have been using are not appropriate for use in the United Kingdom will need to be equipped with alternative methods if they are to continue to maintain discipline and appropriate boundaries. With the G family, establishing ways in which John's parents could routinely offer him approval and affirmation for his efforts to do well proved sufficient to bring about a lessening in the sort of behaviour that had been getting him into trouble. With some other families referred to the project, it has been necessary to help parents find different methods of using their authority when children have presented with challenging behaviour.

Reinforcing change: working with other agencies

With the G family, despite positive changes at home following the commencement of work by the project (John stopped wetting his bed, and his behaviour at home became easier for his parents to manage), he continued to get into trouble at school. As mentioned above, his parents felt that this was because of the sort of reputation he had acquired at school, and that now, even though John was being no naughtier than other children, he would get into trouble with teachers more often. When project workers visited the school, they found John sitting outside the head teacher's office, looking very sorry for himself, in trouble once more for misbehaving in the classroom. Project workers have found that *it is necessary to engage with other agencies involved in order to ensure that positive changes in family life are acknowledged and reinforced.*

While the head teacher saw John's behaviour as unchanged, his classroom teacher confirmed to some extent at least John's parents' view. He had noticed improvements in John's behaviour over the course of the previous term that he felt others in the school had thus far failed to notice. Although he had attempted to bring such changes to the attention of the head teacher and other more senior staff, he felt that as a new teacher his voice did not carry sufficient authority to get across the news of this difference. White and Epston (1990) have written about the way in which a "dominant story" about what a person is like can become so influential that exceptions—moments that demonstrate that a person can sometimes be different—do not get noticed. They have suggested that if an audience can be recruited to notice and applaud small examples of change, this will encourage the amplification of such changes and the emergence of a new "dominant story" about that person.

Accordingly, the project team proposed that a new initiative should be attempted in school in order to change the negative cycle of events whereby John was only ever getting to see his head teacher when he was in some sort of trouble. It was suggested that for a trial period every day, his teacher should find an opportunity to send John to the head teacher to tell her about something that he had done particularly well. The educational psychologist responsible for the school was notified of this intervention, so that she could support its maintenance if necessary during her visits to the school. The suggestion seemed to help, in that over the ensuing weeks and months a "new story" about John emerged at the school, in which he was credited for improving both his behaviour in the classroom and his concentration on his work. This new view of John served also to boost his own self-esteem as a boy who could do well at school and improved relationships between teachers at the school and John's parents.

In order for this intervention to be attended to within the school, it was necessary for the project team to have credibility. In establishing such credibility, it seemed important that both a black African child-protection worker and a white child mental-health worker were co-working together. The black African child-protection worker could speak with authority about the careful assessment of the family that she had undertaken, about the changes that had taken place, and about the importance of raising the self-esteem of black children in order to help them succeed in the United Kingdom. The white child mental-health worker could speak with authority about ways of changing children's behaviour and view of themselves, in a way that school staff were accustomed to pay some attention to. School staff are used to approaching child mental-health workers for advice about the reasons behind children's behaviour and about ways of changing it.

78   PRACTICE PERSPECTIVES

Addressing racial difference with other agencies

It has been the experience of project workers that negative cycles of interaction between school staff and African parents are common among referrals to the project. School staff will often see such parents as punitive and/or neglectful towards their children and as uncooperative in collaborating over ways of resolving difficulties that children are presenting in school. Parents will see school staff as discriminating against their children, complaining unnecessarily about their behaviour, and holding them unfairly accountable for things their children do at school, when they are outside parental control. Against such a backdrop of mistrust and negative judgements, attempts to coordinate intervention strategies between parents and schools are doomed to failure: the more teachers are seen as making such judgements, the more African parents will fail to support efforts to establish ways of collaborating with them. The more African parents fail to collaborate, the more they will be seen as uncooperative by teachers.

In order to intervene in this negative cycle of interaction, project workers have often needed *to work hard to communicate with parents about the positive intent behind teachers' complaints and their wish that the children should succeed in their education, a goal that is held important by all parties. Project workers have also on occasion needed to make explicit with school staff the importance of racial difference and the possibility that their judgements about parents and families could be seen as racist in nature.* In the case of John, it was argued by project workers that it was particularly important for John as a young black boy to build a more positive self-image, as there are so many influences in U.K. society that would lead him to think badly of himself. Teachers were able to appreciate the importance and urgency of helping him improve his self-image, putting significant new energy into the intervention described above. In the case of another of the African families referred to the project, a white worker was made extremely uncomfortable by a head teacher's behaviour towards both her black African colleague and a black African parent. The project worker, feeling that the head was dismissive and disrespectful towards both, sought a further meeting separately to take this up, pointing out that such behaviour could be seen as racist and suggesting alternative ways of behaving that would be more likely to encourage collaboration. The head was able to take such suggestions on board, making a different sort of approach to the parent concerned and asking her to play a more active role in the running of the school. When approached in this more respectful manner, the parent responded in a more positive manner, and a different sort of cycle of interaction was established. In follow-up interviews carried out after the termination of contact with the project, parents have often spoken about this significant positive change in their relationships with teachers at their children's schools.

Addressing racial difference with client families

White members of the project team have *acknowledged explicitly their difference from African families referred, raising questions throughout the work about the appropriateness and usefulness of the perspective that they have offered.* Rather than offering psychological perspectives about ways of making sense of children's behaviour as though such perspectives should be taken as "truth", such ideas will be offered from a position of hesitancy about their relevance: "I don't know whether this idea makes any sort of sense, but . . ." This position is close to that advocated by Dyche and Zayas (1995) for therapists working across-cultures and described by them as "cultural naiveté".

When white project members have taken responsibility for asking family members about their experience of "being black", this has encouraged open discussion of issues that had previously remained unspoken. For example, two brothers, both at primary school, spoke of their experience of being black at their school and how they felt about not having any black teachers.

In fact, African parents have been particularly appreciative of the way in which white members of the project team have engaged with and provided a listening space for their children. "Wendy made me feel at ease," said one parent in a follow-up interview; "Being nice with the children helped me talk . . . I was surprised at the way my son opened up."

Of course, the presence of a black African worker was also valued enormously by African parents and seen as ensuring that their values and ways of doing things would not be misinterpreted: "Having an African social worker meant that the special value of children in African culture was understood, and the need to bring them up to be strong."

Addressing racial difference between project members

At times, project members have been caught inside the negative cycles of mistrust and negative judgements described above. At these moments, black workers can see the white workers as colluding with racist ways of thinking and acting; white workers, in their turn, can feel that their attempts to find a common ground pass unnoticed. For instance, a white worker attempted to demonstrate respect for an African colleague's special knowledge in a particular area by taking a back seat during an interview, but the African worker saw this as being left to do all the work while the white worker sat in judgement.

Painful as these moments are, we have not been surprised by their occurrence considering both the high emotional intensity of the work we do and the history of the relationships between white and African peoples. *We have found that it is imperative to create space in which to explore the impact of these forces on our relationships and how our relationships affect the work we do with children and their families.*

These can be difficult conversations, in which project members find themselves taking risks in trying to talk openly together about things usually left unsaid. *It is helpful to have different viewpoints represented to mitigate against the possibility of polarization, to include the idea that the parties are basically well-intentioned towards each other, and to keep the focus on the outcomes for the child and family.* So, for instance, the contribution of a third worker on the above issue helped the African worker to recognize how her personal style contributed to her colleague's reticence; while the white worker also recognized that their colleague needed a more active style of support for their joint work.

This work has presented us with opportunities for increased understanding and awareness of how in our relationships with each other we are each positioned by history and racism and has helped us to begin to build bridges across differences in race and culture in order to form good working relationships.

The principle of our work has been that a black African perspective and a white British perspective can add to and enhance one another, in ways that are both exciting and unpredictable and are more effective together than either would be apart. Outcomes in terms of deregistration from the child-protection register have been good and feedback from families who have completed a period of work during the three-year lifetime of the project to date has been almost uniformly positive and appreciative of the contributions of both co-working partners. The project is currently at a point of expansion, with five other workers actively seeing families together. It is hoped that our learning from one another will continue apace, and that the model of work which emerges will have applications in many other contexts.

CHAPTER 6

"Strangers in foreign lands"

Jocelyn Avigad & Jane Pooley

Everyone Sang

Everyone suddenly burst out singing;
And I was filled with such delight
As prisoned birds must find in freedom
Winging wildly across the white
Orchards and dark green fields; on; on; and out of sight.

Everyone's voice was suddenly lifted,
And beauty came like the setting sun.
My heart was shaken with tears, and horror
Drifted away.... O but everyone
Was a bird; and the song was wordless; the singing will never
be done.

Siegfried Sassoon (1919)

This poem speaks to us of the joy of finding new possibilities and connections, the effect of such experiences on memories of earlier traumas and horrors, and the fear that such insight will bring only moments of peace that are tenuously held and may be shattered once again at any moment. It is our experience when working with refugees that the issues raised in the poem are present both for client and therapist.

In this chapter we share our experience of working with a refugee family in an inpatient psychiatric setting. We explore the impact of the work and the dilemmas it raised at a number of levels (self, therapeutic work, the institution, and the wider network). We also want to try to convey to the reader our experience when our personal and professional selves were challenged, often beyond words. And, finally, we explore implications for practice.

One of the ways that we used to make sense of the work and to hold a direction was to keep having conversations with each other and with our colleagues both in the unit and in the community. In order to try to recreate this working process, our commentary here is interspersed with transcriptions of some of our conversations.

Thinking of identity

When working with refugee families, we—both therapists and clients alike—are strangers in foreign lands. We need to find a world where we can stand together as we try to create a shared language and understanding, where we can work together on a shared belief system about the possibilities of relationship and find a way of communicating that makes sense to us both. The task is complex, and yet its potential for creativity and challenge is seductive.

To illustrate the layers of complexity that must be addressed, let us for a moment attempt to deconstruct the word "identity". Here we conceptualize identity as the way in which an individual gains a sense of him/herself through relationships with significant others, over time, and in different contexts. For the refugee, the experience of rapid and often violent change can result in the creation of many more identities than might usually be present. These are likely to include the identity that is present before the trauma; that which is co-constructed at the point of sensing danger; of disaster; of rescue; of asylum seeking; of aloneness; of dislocation and after. Traditionally, therapists thinking about the "refugee identity" tend to be more simplistic and centred around the pre-trauma, trauma, and post-trauma experiences and contexts.

No wonder, then, that there is contained in the therapeutic relationship enormous potential for missing each other in the most genuine attempts to connect. If the therapist's belief is that he or she is talking to the traumatized self of the refugee while for the refugee the talk is likely to be moving backwards and forwards through the different identities, sometimes very rapidly, then finding common ground for the relationship is unlikely.

Another way of describing this process could be to see it as talking to the emerging new identity, which means talking to different voices at different times in quick succession. This can be a challenging endeavour for both client and therapist, as it demands taking risks on both sides by moving into unfamiliar and unconventional territory.

To add another complexity to this map, consider how this behaviour gets described in language. For instance, one professional might see the "not connecting" as a symptom of "craziness" that is in the refugee's head as a result of extreme experiences and thus an indication of pathology or of mental illness. Another might talk about it as a symptom of cultural dislocation and bereavement. A third might see the refugee condition as a tragedy of the human condition and the refugee's response as an indicator of resilience. Alongside all these attempts at explanation and understanding we must place the meaning that the refugee and his or her support systems ascribe to the behaviours. As with the therapists, there will be differences between members based on age, gender, culture, and other such variables.

So intertwined, then, are the beliefs that inform the professional system, the beliefs that inform the refugee system, and the context in which these beliefs exist that to consider one without the other is to know only part of the story that is there to be told and understood.

Our position

Our context is an inpatient psychiatric unit for adolescents. The work draws on a number of different theoretical models in a therapeutic-community milieu where differences are enjoyed and explored. So we both resist the invitation to pathologize refugee status and, at the same time, are mindful that mental ill health might be a consequence of it. Most of all, we subscribe to the perspective that favours providing a context where resilience can be fostered—a context, therefore, that offers containment, safety, nurturing, structure and boundaries, a refuge, a safe haven, and a therapeutic presence of witnessing and paying testimony to.

Setting the scene

"Juan" is now a 17-year-old young man, an Angolan refugee, who at the age of 13 was referred to the adolescent inpatient unit where we worked. He had been living in London for two years. Juan had left Angola as a political refugee and lived for a time with a woman friend of the family in the Congo. It was she who brought Juan, at the age of 11, to London to live with his elder brother, "Carlos". Prior to the political upheaval, Juan's parents had worked as teachers in one of the larger cities. They had moved to live in a small village as land workers when Carlos, their eldest son, became a political dissident and his activities had implications for the family's safety.

What we know of Juan's early history is sparse and was pieced together over time through case records and discussions with Juan, his family, and his network. Of significance to us is that Juan is the youngest of six or seven children. We heard from his brother that he was a "very special child" in the family and was particularly protected by his father. Juan was, over time, able to access early memories of his childhood. These included a number of memories of dangerous times—for instance, when armed guards came into his school and threatened the children with guns and possibly raped some of the female pupils in front of him. His early family life, as he knew it, ended when he witnessed the execution of his father and mother. The murder was apparently an act of reprisal for Carlos's defection from the political party in power to the opposition.

When Juan first came to London, he lived with Carlos in temporary housing. English was not his first language. Lingali was the language of everyday conversation; the family were also fluent in French and Portuguese (the official language of Angola). Juan went to mainstream school but soon became disturbed there. He became aggressive and lashed out when he experienced bullying. He also could not bear loud noise. The extremity of his behaviour led to admission to another inpatient unit for younger children. His treatment in that unit was foreshortened as his aggressive and sexualized behaviour at the time divided the staff team, so that it became impossible for them to contain him. This experience resonates with our own and is a dynamic that often happens in work with families and individuals who have experienced events of extreme trauma. It is in this context that our work began.

Referral stage

At the time of referral we learnt that Juan was a very isolated and withdrawn young man who seldom went out, did very little within the home, and could not bear loud noises, including the television. He was not attending school. We also learnt that Carlos had sent for a woman, Beatrice, from Angola who was soon to become his wife. Access to the family had been very difficult for the local outpatient service. They struggled along with education and social services to engage in any meaningful way with the family.

Reflecting conversation

Jocelyn: "One of the features of this work was how much it taxed us as therapists and made us acknowledge, on reflection, how much we changed some of our usual working structures."

Jane: "Yes, things were different right from the beginning. I remember the weekly referral meetings that were held to talk about the young people we were working with towards admission. I remember my increasing sense of unease and dissatisfaction that the pre-admission work was taking so long. The reasons given by the referral team were valid, in that as a group of professionals we held a belief that the professional and family network needed to be joined with the admission process and with our team if our work was to be useful and would fit into a longer-term care plan."

Jocelyn: "So, for instance, in this case we needed to ensure that a secure base for the weekend was available and that we had telephone communication with the family and channels for communicating with community agencies. This had been difficult to achieve because the Education Department could not see their way to committing themselves to this child until he had been 'treated' and the Social Services Department was going through a period of major change which undermined consistent decision making and planning. We also needed to address and understand as best we could issues of language and culture."

These issues of working together with the network and finding appropriate structures and boundaries in which to place our work with community professionals dominated our thinking and actions all the way through to discharge. We now believe that it is no coincidence that these patterns emerged with this case more starkly than with many others, as they reflect the experience of refugee families who must try to integrate many different identities in order to manage dislocation and relocation without "falling apart". This dynamic needs to be understood and worked with, but it should not be used as an excuse for doing nothing.

Admission

Admission finally happened a number of months later with our team's slow and painful recognition that we had been trying to squeeze this family and child into our Western construct of what "should ideally be", whereas in Juan's best interests we needed to offer him a secure base (Byng-Hall, 1995), however tenuous, and work with the fragmentation in the network.

Juan initially came into the unit quiet and subdued. He was described by staff as a beautiful young man, and many staff, knowing of his history, took a protective position in relation to him. It was not long, however, before Juan began challenging for control, often with both verbal and physical aggression. He started stealing property from adolescents and staff, and at times he would sing at the top of his voice in a disturbing way. The singing highlighted the paradox that Juan presented for us. He had an exceptionally beautiful voice and yet seemed to us to use it as a weapon to intimidate. At the end of each week, Carlos nearly always forgot to collect Juan. It was as if he could not hold Juan in mind. We arranged fares and taxis, but still to no avail. Finally we would have to let Juan go home unaccompanied in a taxi and to return the same way on a Sunday evening. Carlos was happy with this arrangement, as he saw it as appropriate for a boy of Juan's age. Unit staff, in contrast, were left feeling concerned that this practice was unsafe and uncaring. Because the importance of "handing over" was differently prioritized for unit staff and for the family, we were not able to let Juan's family know how Juan had been during the week and we were not able to find out from Carlos how Juan had been at the weekend. It was as if there were a huge void in our working relationships and a gap between the two worlds. Juan, in turn, had to try to bridge this, and our task was to support him to do so. However. he, and we, had to hold in mind that ultimately his home was with his family and his community.

The family presented the unit with another huge dilemma—that of how to engage effectively with them so that family work could complement the work that Juan was doing in the unit. The initial hope was that the family would come to the unit at agreed times with all members attending. Appointments, even when backed up with telephone calls, were not kept, and eventually the team moved their work to the family home in the hope that this might make engagement more possible. Still, Carlos was often not there, and when he was it was obvious that he was preoccupied with issues to do with his asylum-seeking status and settling into work. He found it unbearable to consider what might be disturbing Juan, holding a firm view that Juan was now of an age to be man enough to get on with his life and future as he, Carlos, had done. Talking about the past for Carlos seemed futile, painful, and disturbing.

The challenge for the family workers was at least twofold. On the one hand, we had to redefine our construct of what family work should be in order to both hold on to our belief of the value of the work and at the same time find a fit with the family so that it could have meaning for them too. On the other, we needed to deal with a staff group where splits were emerging between those who felt protective and those who felt that it was time to draw clear boundaries and not make a special case of Juan.

In this climate, the team requested that Juan have some individual work. Staff were becoming increasingly desperate about the unit's ability to help Juan, as well as about the impact that his presence was having on the unit community and on the group process.

Reflecting conversation

Jocelyn: "And I was thinking, Jane, what about the challenge to our thinking about the meaning of therapy for us, and then for us and the family as a system?"

Jane: "I can most easily think about this question in relation to the individual work that I was asked to do with Juan.

"The idea of building a relationship with me appeared, for Juan, to quite fundamentally threaten his existence so that it was almost intolerable for him to know the feelings either of tenderness or fury that were aroused. On the other hand, Juan always remembered when it was time for his session with me and would for periods come and sleep in the chair in my room. I found myself acting in strange and unusual ways, which I then had to spend time thinking and talking about, because—as for you, Jocelyn—my usual structures and boundaries were being challenged. For instance, I started a patchwork quilt in the sessions with Juan, which was perhaps my rather primitive attempt to ritualize my sitting with him while he tried to put the pieces of his life, of his mind, heart and soul, together. It was my way of being together and yet creating a space that did not feel too unbearably intense for Juan. In this act, on reflection, we were quite literally binding together different pieces of cloth and different textures, an act that reflected our endeavour to bring together thoughts and experiences in the room. I also, on occasion, went for walks with Juan at his instigation, as this seemed to create a tolerable environment of movement and space both to be together and to be separate. On one of these walks we came to a high fence, which Juan gleefully helped me climb over!

"Around this time a conflict emerged between myself and some of the unit staff whose expectation was that individual work would be about post-traumatic stress debriefing and the consequent emergence of Juan's 'true' story.

"Unit staff were preoccupied with an idea that if only they knew Juan's full story, then they would be able to work with him more easily. I, on the other hand, was adamant that my work with Juan was not to find out the 'truth' of his experience but to understand his needs through what might emerge in the relationship between us. I also held the view that the experience of being unconditionally 'held' was vital for Juan if he was to develop and rediscover his capacity to think."

Jocelyn: "What do you think of the idea that this became even more apparent when he began to access his memories of his parents before their deaths and then through their deaths to after?"

Jane: "It became apparent that, as Juan was able more and more to contemplate the trauma that led to his being dislocated, a parallel process was going on for him in relation to significant relationships and attachments that he was developing in the unit. As the feelings that were aroused became more unbearable, he needed to distance himself, often in a violent and aggressive way, from relationships in the unit. Just prior to this time, Juan had been involved in extreme stealing behaviour on the unit. This seemed to embody his conflict between the past and present and the anxiety that was aroused, resulting in his attacking what he was experiencing at some level as good and wholesome.

"The first quilt ended on a funeral fire that Juan wished to arrange, having made a clay plaque in his art-therapy session to commemorate the memory of his parents. He lit a fire and invited unit members to share this with him. This ritual marked a movement in the work with Juan. It was as if his past and present worlds were able to come together for that moment. Juan's presentation of himself began to slowly change. He took an interest in the next quilt and wanted to choose which material would be sown in each time."

Jocelyn: "Your reflections are making me remember the unit trip to Wales that he and I went on around this time. During this trip we connected very strongly because of our shared African backgrounds, and so when we looked together at the landscape in Wales we thought about the African landscape and how similar it was. Not long after that, Juan began stealing and becoming violent on the trip and had to be sent home."

Jane: "I remember that you, Jocelyn, were anxious at this time that Juan might be on the verge of a psychotic breakdown."

Jocelyn: "That is absolutely right, and I had forgotten just how anxious I was and how much of a struggle I was having inside myself. That was the conflict between the personal and professional parts of me wanting to take Juan home with me and wanting to have him in my family and knowing how impossible this was. Another conflict was around the ethical issue of the treatment being a risky business, both for Juan and also for those of us working and living with him. Was I justified in taking such risks?"

So these were some of the issues that emerged in our work with Juan and his family. There were many more, but we have chosen to highlight these few as they seem to reflect the central dilemmas that are often thrown up when working with this client group. It is also our belief that focusing on the process is more important than paying too much attention to the detail of the story. We now consider what we might learn from the experience of this piece of work.

Thoughts for practice

One of the most difficult tasks has been making connections between the experience of working with Juan and the theoretical thinking that has underpinned the work. Sometimes we have succeeded, and sometimes not so well. This we have now come to understand is, at least in part, what it must be like for Juan himself in his attempts to access and integrate himself into a foreign world. Sometimes he can draw on familiar structures, experiences, and wisdoms to help him on his way, but many times he must grope in the dark.

No wonder the Greek origin of the word "text" is so appealing. Its meaning is "weaving", and thus "context" can be seen as the weaving together of many threads. In the case of a refugee family trying to survive, it is precisely these many contextual threads of identity and experience that have to be woven into some sort of patchwork whole: experiences and identities that predate the trauma, those that are part of it, and, still more, those that are embedded in the subsequent dislocation and relocation processes.

For the therapists, too, there are so many dissonances and complexities to manage. For instance, there is the dissonance between Juan's inner and outer worlds and how this is reflected in the splits within the staff team. There are the transitions Juan must be helped to make between at least two worlds—the Western therapeutic world of an inpatient unit and that of the family, which in this case was rooted in the culture of African Angola, a country in the midst of a violent and destructive struggle. Also, there is the feeling that whatever you do can never be enough, because, like the message contained in the "Humpty-Dumpty" nursery rhyme, nothing can ever put it back together again the way it was. Then there is the "almost-not-spoken" question: "If I do allow myself to be open to the intimacy of the therapeutic relationship, will I be placing myself at risk of being violated or even destroyed because of the powerful nature of the refugee's hopes and expectations which places me in an impossible position?" On the one hand, hope is contained in the belief that the therapist can solve all the different problems; on the other, despair is inevitable when facing the impossibility of this task. Unspeakable, maybe, but left unspoken at what cost?

What else did we learn? In working with the individual, the family, and the network, as long as we kept in mind that engagement is a process and not a discrete act we were able to achieve many things. For instance, we were able to help Carlos and Juan to deconstruct their memories (and flashbacks) and stories of their time before, during, and after the murder. We were also able to help them construct a family genogram, which for Juan was a journey of new discoveries—for instance, that he had two sisters that he said he did not know about. However, we are left with the idea that the story that emerged may or may not be the "truth". Perhaps it matters not, as the need to survive requires a coherent and jointly owned story on which to anchor present and future living. It is possible, though, that by Juan having to tell a story that may not have been based on reality, he might have experienced an extreme degree of conflict and disturbance. For the therapist not to be too reverent to a particular story is well documented in the literature.

We learnt that planning transitions carefully, allowing a lot of time to support Juan with his anxiety about the new and unknown, was vital if he was to be able to use opportunities.

The feature of this case, and of our experience of working with other refugees, is not that any of the issues above are not part of good practice in any case, but that the intensity and need to attend to the dynamics in careful and thoughtful detail is heightened and demands strong commitment and tenacity. The extreme feelings that the team and individual workers might experience are likely to include isolation, splitting, fury, impotence, and fear. It is vital that there are structures in place in which these feelings can be held, thought through, and not personalized or acted upon.

As for Juan, his road continues to be a rocky one. Our work formally ended with him when he left the unit to return to live with Carlos. He went to a pupil-referral unit, where he learnt and achieved much, including some GCSEs and a range of social and survival skills. However, at the point that he was preparing to leave the structure of the pupil-referral unit there was upheaval at home, and Juan resorted to familiar, violent ways of dealing with and communicating fear, distress, and anger. He was part of a group that attacked a youth, and he received a three-year prison sentence for this. From prison, Juan has been in touch. He wants to remember some of the learning he did with us, particularly about the possibility of different futures that he might be capable of having and his part in whether they happen or not. For client and professional, the dilemma and risk inherent in the work—past, present, and future—is: "How much is too much?"

No easy road

Not easy departing loved ones,
Far away stranded in an alien world.
With a promise that a new day shall bring a new tomorrow,
Even though there are painful mountains to climb,
And sometimes things are not what they seem.
Be courageous for a new tomorrow,
Life is not an empty dream.
In the dawn, a new set of footprints
Seeing, shall take heart again.
No easy road, no easy road,
My mother told me.

[Written in 1995 by Agostinho Mbala, an Angolan man living in south London]

CHAPTER 7

Visible differences: individual and collective risk-taking in working cross-culturally

Shila Khan

Cross-cultural work poses many challenges to therapists, trainers, trainees, supervisors, and institutions alike. Discussions about how to attend to these issues—whether in therapy, training, or supervision or in relation to the life of organizations—can often engender individual feelings of vulnerability, anxiety, confusion, dissonance, and guardedness. Moreover, there may also be a collective and institutional unwillingness, whether wittingly or unwittingly, to delve into what can be experienced as the uncertain and unsafe terrain of race and culture. These individual and institutional reactions can often stifle the possibility of creative and constructive dialogue around these issues.

Recently, however, there has been an acknowledgement of the importance of attending to the socio-economic and political contexts, such as class, poverty, and culture, affecting individual experiences and the institutions that they inhabit. This has partly come about as a result of certain key debates in wider society, such as those on citizenship and social exclusion. A significant development in the United Kingdom in the area of race and cultural issues has been the Macpherson Report (1999), which has highlighted the damaging impact of racism on people's lives and the need to create a legislative framework within which individuals and institutions are required to take responsibility to reduce racially discriminatory practices. Additionally, other attempts such as various publications, policy documents, ethical guidelines regulating the practice and training of psychotherapy (including family therapy), conferences, and changes to some course structures have been made to address issues of race, culture, and antidiscriminatory practices.

In the field of family therapy, recent paradigm shifts towards adopting a postmodern and social-constructionist perspective have given birth to different ways of conceptualizing and practising therapy. For instance, the idea that relationships between people are socially embedded within certain socio-political contexts such as gender, race, culture, and class has changed the view of therapy, and of the therapist, as no longer being neutral but influenced by these experiences and as influencing the therapeutic relationship. Postmodern ideas have challenged notions of ultimate truths and, instead, have given way to discourses about the existence of multiple world views, and an emphasis in therapy on understanding how people create meanings about their experiences through language. Yet these theoretical developments seem to have made little visible difference in cross-cultural practices, with few exceptions, so that one is left to wonder whether some of these gestures, although well intentioned, are perhaps more in the form of an enshrined ideal rather than an operationalized reality.

As a family therapist who is Asian, and having arrived as an immigrant from Bangladesh with her family twenty-seven years ago, I have my own experiences of encountering and navigating between different cultural frames. These frames arise from simultaneously being in the culture I have left behind in my country of origin, the culture I am located within of the host country, the culture I came with at the point of entry into the new country, and the culture I am creating, which is in essence a fusion of my ongoing relationship with all of these experiences. It is like weaving a patchwork quilt from these myriad and varied experiences, which on their own are different from each other but as a whole make a coherent and aesthetically pleasing pattern. The vibrant threads of my own cultural heritage have formed a tapestry within which have been woven strands from other cultural heritages.

Perhaps these experiences of weaving in and out of different cultural frames, and weaving together different cultural narratives and experiences, partly account for why as a family therapist I am particularly interested in how cultural differences affect the therapeutic relationship and the process of therapy. The dual experiences of being an outsider by virtue of holding my own cultural identity and ethnicity, while at the same time being able to enter into and be a part of other cultural experiences, perhaps lend themselves particularly well to this area of work, where one has to switch between levels while at the same time attempting to build some sense of coherence between the levels. My being grounded in my own culture has meant that I have been able to take risks in experimenting with and at times even incorporating values and practices from the host culture.

These personal experiences and identities are useful tools in my professional work as a family therapist, based in a child and adolescent mental health service in cosmopolitan London. Here, one is working with clients from a diversity of cultural and socioeconomic backgrounds, who themselves are grappling to bring about some coherence to different, often conflicting, narratives about their lives. The complexity of issues encountered in cross-cultural work is not helped by the paucity of literature in family therapy pertaining to this work. From the few exceptions that are to be found (e.g. Burck & Speed, 1995; Carter & McGoldrick, 1989; Fernando, 1995a; Kareem & Littlewood, 1992; Krause, 1998; Lau, 1988, 2000; McGoldrick, 1998; Perelberg & Miller, 1990), what has emerged is that such work can become an emotional and intellectual minefield—often challenging and highly charged for both the therapist and the client. Anecdotally, practitioners often refer to this kind of work as being fraught with muddles and mistakes, where there is often a sense of dissatisfaction, discomfort, therapeutic impasse, or paralysis.

In this chapter, I am interested in looking at the practices that can constrain or liberate cross-cultural therapeutic work. What enables or facilitates practitioners to take risks by giving up positions of relative certainty, familiarity, and sameness in order to engage with different frames of thinking and doing? What enables them to do this, both in relation to themselves and their clients, in ways that make visible and meaningful differences? Moreover, how can individual risk-taking be supported and maintained by the agencies or institutions in which the therapist is working so that these practices become a collective endeavour rather than isolated struggles? How might training institutions create and maintain the kind of climate and conditions to enable practitioners in training, and institutions themselves, to think more creatively in relation to these issues? The main aim of this chapter is to provoke curiosity and invite self-reflexivity rather than to provide answers. In addition, I refer to some clinical material to illustrate the subtleties, dilemmas and challenges of working cross-culturally and interculturally.

Encountering cultures: whose culture?

Culture can be defined as a set of beliefs, customs, ideas, sentiments, institutions, and achievements that are internalized and externalized in varying degrees by a group of people, which in turn regulate and guide thoughts, conduct, practices, and social and personal relationships. Culture is, therefore, represented by "a group of persons who share particular interpretations of the world because of reasons of geography, gender, religion, and other contingencies that play a role in lending a degree of homogeneity to their perspectives" (Paré, 1996, p. 25).

One of the reasons why cultural issues have, until recently, remained in the margins of systemic theory, training, and practice may be to do with the culture of the institutions themselves, which are in the main predominantly white and middle class. Perhaps the assumption in these institutions is that there is little or no cultural diversity among white people, thereby relegating such issues to a place of less importance. Clearly, such a view is erroneous if not unjust to the diversity that exists among the lives of people sharing the same racial background or skin colour. The idea that variations occur within the same cultural group is often overlooked or forgotten. For instance, a white person from Yorkshire, England, will be different in many respects from a white person from Amsterdam, Holland. The misconception is that white people have a shared culture, which is the same. However, it is understandable as a response where the visible sameness of being physically white makes invisible certain differences that clearly exist between people from the same racial group.

It is interesting to note that in family therapy training institutions in the United Kingdom considerable progress has been made in addressing gender issues. Perhaps the substantial presence of articulate and strong women in these institutions may account for why gender as a visible difference, rather than culture, has been a privileged issue for scrutiny and change. Although there are no available statistics, anecdotal evidence and personal experience suggests that family therapy institutions have successfully employed European ethnic minorities as family therapy teachers and practitioners but very few from the black and Asian communities. This lack of presence of black and Asian family therapists in most family therapy institutions in Great Britain may be another factor behind these institutions absenting themselves from making continuous and significant progress in issues to do with race and culture.

There may be other factors constraining the development of creative cross-cultural practices. For example, the ways in which discourses about culture are spoken about give the impression that culture is associated with certain ethnic groups only, and as belonging to others rather than something we all have. Perhaps there is an idea that issues to do with race and culture, as with class, disability, and sexuality, are matters concerning the minority other and therefore not of concern for everyone. This perception often results in the view that work with certain ethnic groups is a form of speciality, requiring special knowledge, skills, and training, something that only certain therapists from certain cultures can do. Indeed, this form of thinking currently means that certain therapists from certain ethnic groups are often invited in their position as cultural consultants or experts to provide assessments, opinions, therapy, and training for particular ethnic groups. Undoubtedly, such work does require therapists to have some degree of knowledge of the cultural background of the client, as well as sensitivity and respect for the needs of the clients. However, to see intercultural work as only something that certain people can do is to risk separation and marginalization of such work from the mainstream practice of family therapy.

Perhaps one way of making a difference in this work is to see all therapeutic exchanges as essentially an encounter between two, or more, cultures—that of the therapist and the client(s). This may be a way to avoid exoticizing and marginalizing this work and bring it more to the realm of what therapists should be capable of doing. This suggestion has been made by other authors: for instance, Burman, Gowrisunkur, and Sangha (1998) suggest a

> need to see all therapy as intercultural, with each party therein (including the theoretical framework and setting, as well as the person of the therapist) bearing culture—rather than culture being a presumed attribute only of black people, thus perpetuating the projections and displacement of responsibility for addressing issues of "race" and culture onto black people (as receivers and providers of services). [p. 232]

Another author has proposed that one of the consequences of a paradigm shift towards postmodern thinking is that "the central metaphor of families as systems is now being subsumed by a view that construes families and other clients as interpretative communities, or storying cultures" (Paré, 1995, p. 2). A corollary of this would be an emphasis on the cultural values and experience of the therapist as well as the clients and on the impact of the interplay between the two on the therapeutic relationship.

Such ways of thinking have emerged from recent significant developments in the family therapy field brought on by postmodern and social-constructionist perspectives. For instance, currently in family therapy training there is a focus on exploring the personal self of the therapist, in particular how individual experiences, values, and ways of seeing the world impact on the professional self of the therapist. Yet again, from the little that has been written in this area, the indications are that there is insufficient attention to the issues of culture in the personal and professional development of therapists, and that training institutions can do more to help ground therapists in relation to these issues (Hildebrand, 1998).

Another constraint may be to do with the words used to describe certain cultural groups. For instance, the words "ethnic minority" conjure up images of a small, lesser, other compared with and different from a main another. There is a sense of one group (the minority) being seen in the context of another (the majority), often with an emphasis on the differences between the two. These differences across the two groups—such as skin colour, dress, diet, cultural norms and practices, beliefs, rules for social engagement and interactions, and access to resources such as money, employment, and political power—impact in subtle and obvious ways on the relationships between individuals from these groups. What is often overlooked are the similarities between and across these groups, such as parental love, the significance of marriage and family, having to cope with the death of a loved one, to name but a few.

I would argue that this process of overemphasizing cultural differences while relegating similarities might be another obstacle to creative cross-cultural work. It reinforces the notion of an unknown other and provokes anxieties about getting things wrong, or being seen as racist, incompetent, or politically incorrect, thus making it difficult to maintain a stance of curiosity. This is illustrated in the following case:

> A white female social worker was discussing with an Asian female colleague her work with an Asian young woman. The client had been sexually abused as a child by a male family friend and, in adulthood, physically and sexually abused by two subsequent partners. In one session, the client said to the social worker, "All Asian men are violent—it is their culture." The social worker had not responded to this comment in the session, and she expressed her unease about not doing so to her colleague. In the course of their discussion, it became apparent to the social worker that although she could understand why the client had made a generalization about Asian men, given her individual experiences of abuse by them, she felt paralysed to explore the meaning behind what was, essentially, also a prejudiced view about Asian men and Asian culture. The Asian colleague asked what difference it would have made if a white client had made such a comment—that all white men were violent because of their culture. She commented that with the white client she would have been more familiar with the culture and therefore in a position to develop conversations about these generalizations and perhaps even

challenge them over the course of her work with the client. In the absence of such knowledge, the worker felt it might appear disrespectful to the client to challenge aspects of the client's comments pertaining to her culture.

In this example, it is important to highlight that the cultural differences between the therapist and the client did not impede the development of a good therapeutic relationship between the two, nor did it impair the work that needed to be done. It is merely an example of how being a stranger or being unfamiliar with the culture of the client can sometimes silence curiosity and risk-taking in the therapeutic relationship and process. A similar process can occur when therapists encounter clients from their own ethnic background. For instance, some white colleagues have remarked that they rarely ask their white clients questions about their culture, assuming it to be the same as theirs. Difference and sameness in the cultures of the therapist and the client can sometimes act to "shut down" conversations about culture, often in ways that are subtle and difficult to monitor.

The following example illustrates how cultural sameness between the therapist and client can sometimes impose obstacles to creative thinking:

An Asian therapist had been seeing a 16-year-old Asian girl, who had been sexually abused at the age of 10 years by a male relative. Having talked about the abuse in the middle phase of therapy, the young woman wanted to talk with the therapist about ways to gain control over her studies, as this was an area that she would often relinquish control over and would consequently fall behind. She was undoubtedly bright and had ambitions to go to university, especially in order for her to have some sense of independence and self-agency in the future. A student from Italy joined the Asian therapist for a one-off session. Her focus of interest was about whether this young woman would have an arranged marriage and eliciting her views about this possibility. In posing this question to the client, a very significant conversation took place with the client about her fears of having to marry someone she would not necessarily know very well, and how she would cope with having to be intimate, especially sexually, with a stranger. She was able to make connections between her sense of helplessness arising from her childhood abuse and her fears of being in an adult sexual relationship in the future.

This example shows how cultural sameness can sometimes filter out certain areas for therapeutic exploration, whereas cultural difference may allow for curiosity to develop new tracks of conversation, which may be therapeutically significant. Both the clinical examples demonstrate other ways of generating creativity in one's work—that is, by involving other colleagues to view and discuss one's work, in order to elicit other ways of thinking and intervening. An important aspect of such reflections may be to enquire how cultural sameness and difference can act to both constrain and liberate the therapist in her or his relationship with the client and the process of therapy. Both cultural similarities and differences are therefore essential ingredients to the process of therapy and in establishing a good-enough relationship for effective and meaningful therapeutic work.

Similarities provide a way to make connections; thus, a sole attention to differences may create further distance between the therapist and client. Conversely, an overemphasis on the similarities or sameness may exclude certain significant differences. One of the tasks for the therapist is to introduce what Bateson (1972) refers to as "news of a difference" and "a difference that makes a difference" to the client's way of thinking. It is suggested, therefore, that a way to enrich the therapeutic relationship and broaden the repertoire of therapeutic choices is for the therapist to hold in mind both the differences and the similarities between and within different cultural groups, and between the therapist and client.

Knowing and not knowing

Both therapist and client enter into the therapeutic process knowing and not knowing certain things, and they have to create pathways to proceed from a state of not knowing to one of increased knowledge about the other. This is especially true of the therapist, who has to make more effort to engage the client as well as familiarize him/herself with the complex landscape that constitutes the client's world. This task is made more difficult when the therapist encounters clients from different ethnic groups, where the cultural differences are greater. Here again, current systemic training does not fully equip the therapist to meet the challenges of such encounters. In training, for instance, it is not always possible for the therapist to experience working with families from a range of ethnic backgrounds and thus use these as a reference point later when encountering families from different cultures.

Also, the theory that is taught does not often encompass information about different family forms in other ethnic groups, so that at the end of training there can be a lack of knowledge about the lives of people who come from different cultures. In training, personal and professional development modules do not necessarily delve deep into eliciting the cultural biases and stereotypes that trainees come with, so that they often leave training with many of these preconceptions unchallenged and invisible—perhaps even unknown to the trainee. Many courses pay attention to helping trainees become aware of the changing nature of white British families and the values underpinning individual and familial lives. There is, however, very little mentioned about the changing nature of families in other cultures, or of the culture itself.

For instance, Asian families may often be talked about in relation to certain stereotypical themes, such as arranged marriage, cultural conflict between first and second generation, and oppressive environments for women. While some of these experiences may be borne out in some Asian families, there is a danger that they are seen as being representative and constitutive experiences of all Asian families for all time. As with white British families, Asian families in Britain have also undergone many socio-economic changes, which have transformed certain aspects of their cultural beliefs and practices. For instance, the dominant trend towards many Asians living in nuclear rather than extended families, an increasing number of mixed-race marriages and children with dual or multiple heritages, and the wide range of ethnic-identity descriptions are a few examples of such changes and transitions in the Asian communities.

Thus, training and therapy would benefit considerably by paying more attention to the socio-economic and cultural contexts of these communities—in particular, the changing nature of family forms and relationships, beliefs, religious, and cultural practices. Additionally, it is important to keep in mind that, as with the term "British", the terms "Asian", "black", "Irish", "Chinese", or "African-Caribbean" each refer to a diverse group of people with variations in regional backgrounds, dialects and language, class, education, and how they see themselves in relation to cultural and religious affiliations. To do justice to the diversity of experiences it would be important to engage with and elicit these unique aspects of individual and family lives. This would include keeping in mind that families themselves are the coming together of different cultural experiences and interpretations and that in any one family there be a range of cultural beliefs, practices, and descriptions about identity.

Cultural exchanges: transparency and using one's prejudices creatively

As mentioned previously, there are several creative ideas in family therapy already that lend themselves to facilitating cross-cultural work. One such idea is to see the therapist, the therapeutic relationship, and the process of therapy as being embedded within wider socio-political discourses and influenced by the constructions and world views of the therapist and client. This view of the therapist suggests that therapy is an exchange of interpretations rather than knowledge between the therapist and the client. Thus, "the therapist cannot know the meanings attributed by the client to his or her actions, . . . in an objective way, but it is through hypothesizing . . . that they construct the therapeutic context" (Fruggeri, 1992, p. 46). The very self and identity of the therapist, both personal and professional, then become the tools for crafting the therapeutic relationship.

Essentially, this involves the therapist having constant and rigorous conversations both with him/herself as to how he or she is participating in the relationship with the client, as well as with the client to check things out and encourage feedback about the process of therapy and the therapeutic relationship. In cross-cultural work, it may be particularly useful if the therapist can be transparent with the client about his or her own cultural experiences and preferred narratives, and with what he or she may "know" about the culture of the client as a way to invite the client's comments as to whether these accounts fit for him or her or not. For instance, the therapist may locate him/herself within gendered and cultural narratives to pose questions of the client in ways that expand rather than narrow conversations. One example of this type of question has been developed by Barry Mason, which he refers to as the "Not the Miracle Question"; this is a way of exploring what would be happening if things were going wrong, in whichever context one was interested in addressing. In a cross-cultural therapeutic encounter, the therapist may utilize such a question by saying, for instance, "As a white male therapist from Leeds, what would I be thinking or saying to you, as an Asian male brought up in Bradford, to get things wrong about you?" This kind of stance on the part of the therapist can convey a respectful and genuine wish to hear from the client's perspective while at the same time initiate conversations about the idea of finding a workable fit between the client and the therapist, despite their differences and preferred ways of thinking.

Such an interaction of values and positions in the therapeutic encounter has been eloquently teased out by one set of authors, who suggest that "Therapy occurs in the interplay of the prejudices of therapist and client—a cybernetics of prejudices" (Cecchin et al., 1994, p. 8). Seeing therapy with this particular lens, they elaborate on how this can change the way therapists relate to their clients:

> Rather than search for correctness, what is important is to consider how our own prejudices fit, are affected by, and interfere with the hierarchy of prejudices and actions of our clients.... If therapists can view their models, hypotheses, and techniques as prejudices rather than unquestionable facts, they are less likely simply to attempt to force these biases on to others. Rather, they are more likely to engage in open dialogue with others about the implications of different biases. [p. 15]

Although the concept sounds simple, putting it into practice requires some skill so that the prejudices shared by the therapist are not conveyed as facts but as a way to invoke curiosity about the preferences of the client.

Another related and useful concept is that of irreverence (Cecchin, Lane, & Ray, 1992). Again, this term refers to the position a therapist may take in engaging with the client. Thus, it is suggested that,

> The irreverent therapist is sceptical towards polarities, thereby affording himself freedom from both the passive position of, "I must not go in and introduce an idea about how people can change", and the strategic position of, "I've got to come up with a tactic". With irreverence the therapist introduces an idea but does not necessarily believe that people should follow it.
>
> Just as it is impossible not to communicate, it is also impossible not to have a hypothesis. Why should a therapist try to control a desire to formulate a hypothesis, an idea? Instead, why not utilize this notion to maximum benefit? As long as he does not fall in love with the hypothesis, as long as he plays with it, or talks to colleagues about it, there appears to be no valid argument to prevent him from building a hypothesis. The therapist can take responsibility for his feeling or guess, yet be willing to discard the idea when it is no longer useful. He can use hypotheses as descriptions rather than as explanations. [Cecchin et al., 1992, p. 10]

Being irreverent as a therapist means that one can question and be curious about one's own preferred ideas and those of the clients. So, the therapist may say something to this effect : "In my family we do X because we think this is important for our family life. I am finding it difficult to understand how in your family you have chosen to do Y. Can you help me to understand why this practice is of particular importance to you?" Such a track of enquiry would still allow the therapist to have conversations with the client about entertaining alternative ways of thinking and behaving, which is an important aspect of therapy, including cross-cultural work.

Another significant tool for aiding this work can be taken from recent developments in ways of conceptualizing the therapeutic relationship. The idea that the therapeutic relationship is embedded in wider socio-cultural discourses has been developed to include the more intimate dimensions of the therapeutic relationship (Flaskas & Perlesz, 1996). These focus on the usefulness of certain psychoanalytic ideas in understanding the process of therapy, the therapeutic relationship between the client and the therapist, and the processes impacting on the way the therapist participates in various interactions with the client.

An important concern to these proponents, and one that is crucial in cross-cultural work, too, is the dynamic of power between therapist and client. For instance, Jones (1994) draws attention to the issue of power in the therapeutic relationship and the need for therapists to be constantly vigilant as to whether this is being used appropriately or abused. She suggests that,

> Behaving ethically ... also means bearing in mind that one's current stance is contingent and open to re-assessment; that one's own perceptions are always and inevitably subjective, historically and contextually influenced, selective and (paradoxically) elective. In other words, although our views are open to many influences we also hold responsibility for them. [p. 161]

This raises issues about the onus on the therapist to be accountable and rigorous in her or his practice and thinking. As Fruggeri (1992) states : "In this light it is not a mere matter of principle that therapists are responsible for their power of construction. The power of construction emerges as a responsibility that is scientific and, at the same time, ethical and social" (p. 51).

Indeed, these skills in self-reflection, self-reflexivity, being vigilant with one's thinking and practice, maintaining a stance of curiosity and respect, inviting scrutiny about our thinking and practice from our clients and colleagues, and keeping in mind the sociocultural processes underpinning one's relationship with clients are the essential tools for creative cross-cultural work.

Individual and collective responsibility: creative opportunities for enhanced practice

How can individuals be encouraged to take therapeutic risks in working with clients from cultural backgrounds different from their own? One way is to see all therapeutic encounters as an exchange of cultures and therefore an act of interpretation between the world views and experiences of the therapist and the client. Therapists can, therefore, take on this work utilizing the resources, skills, sensitivities, and competencies they already possess as a therapist rather than feeling de-skilled to do this work. Another asset would be to acquire some amount of knowledge of the cultural norms and practices of different cultural groups and then to use these creatively to open up conversations rather than as a rigid frame of reference for all families from that group.

Training institutions are in a good position to change existing aspects of their course structure and content in such a way as to enable future therapists to develop their thinking and practice in cross-cultural work. Practitioners can seek support in this work through consultation with colleagues both within and outside their agencies.

Being curious about one's own thinking and behaviour in the therapeutic domain and that of one's clients, as well as paying attention to the sociocultural dimensions affecting the relationship, including experiences of discrimination and racism, are important elements of doing this work. Wider paradigmatic shifts in family therapy have begun to offer additional ways of conceptualizing and being active in the therapeutic relationship and the process of therapy. For instance, the integration of certain key psychoanalytic concepts, attachment theory, an anthropological perspective, and socio-economic and cultural dimensions organizing people's lives have been major developments. These strands of thinking have enabled therapists to simultaneously acknowledge the integrity of the therapeutic encounter as both an intimate relationship between two or more people, mediated by individual experiences and interpretations, as well as by wider public and societal discourses and practices. Thus, the challenge for family therapists is to keep in mind both the micro- and the macro-dimensions affecting our relationship with our clients.

Another challenge is for us as therapists to become increasingly more aware of how we, as individuals and institutions, are positioning ourselves in relation to our clients from different cultural backgrounds. Some progress has been made, but, undoubtedly, family therapy as a discipline and an institution needs to take more risks in enhancing existing ways of working cross- and interculturally. As practitioners, it would be useful for us to share our successes, dilemmas, confusions, and muddles, not only with our clients but also with each other, in order to create a relatively safe context where we can take risks to engage and grapple with our differences in ways that make a visible difference.

CHAPTER 8

A risky balance: striving to merge professional white issues and personal black issues

Gella Richards

First, I would like to put this chapter into a context to help the reader understand how I came to present a workshop that took place at the 1999 Institute of Family Therapy (IFT) conference. This context-setting involves selecting autobiographical details to help the reader understand where I am coming from. I also present clinical material to demonstrate how strong feelings from a case led me to develop the workshop. One of the workshop's exercises is described, together with some feedback from the participants. I conclude the chapter with my personal recommendations.

When I was invited to write this chapter, I found myself facing my own personal dilemma. I was asked to be honest, to state my motivation and feelings for running such a workshop and to explore some of the risks I had taken. Initially, this seemed straightforward: after all, I had shared all of this with the workshop participants. However, the main difference was that it had been verbal and had been shared among a group of professionals who I believed respected confidentiality. I felt that in that environment, participants had been less judgemental; the atmosphere had been one of wanting to share with like-minded people experiences of dilemmas, risk-taking, and learning from each other. In that context, the words took on more of an "evaporated" quality, in that ideas were discussed and built upon and misunderstandings clarified. The process involved initial individual ideas and concepts being negotiated to produce shared ideas and concepts.

Background and orientation

My main training has been in psychology, though I have studied family therapy and systemic modules at Master's level; my clinical practice has involved working with families, using systemic models.

Using family therapy techniques, and the issues that arise from working systemically, has always fascinated me. During my training as a psychologist, I found that the focus on individualistic ways of understanding clients' problems was in many cases limiting because it often did not take account of the clients' context or the relationships *between* relationships. In many cases for people from ethnic-minority backgrounds, context emphasizes extended-family networks. A major advantage of the systemic approach is that it sees the family as not only a unit, but made up of many subsystems (Boyd-Franklin, 1989). It also recognizes that the family is a system within larger systems and that it contributes to other systems. This recognition of interdependence means that the approach in many cases is well placed to at least raise awareness and work with the processes of other systems, which influence subsystems within the family and, ultimately, the family as a whole. It is not uncommon for some of the systems to rely on routine protocols that perpetuate oppressive practices. Obvious conventions are those that create the opportunity for racism (Burke, 1997). So, unlike many of the individualistic approaches, a systemic approach may acknowledge racist practices as part and parcel of the system and hence as a context in which ethnic minorities and their families have to strive to exist.

Particular dilemmas seemed to arise when I was working in a residential family unit towards the end of my training.

A RISKY BALANCE 113

The dilemmas begin and the first risk is taken

One of the difficulties in writing this chapter is that I am aware that there is a dearth of ethnic-minority professionals working in the field of psychotherapy, family therapy, and psychology. Hence, rightly or wrongly, when I as an ethnic-minority professional commit something to paper it may be seen as representative of ethnic-minority professionals in general. I may be seen, especially by my "community", as an *"ambassador* for my people". In ethnic-minority communities, an ambassador presents just the strengths and the successes and does not "betray" the community by revealing difficulties, weaknesses, and struggles to the outside world. However, in this chapter, I want to start my risk-taking by considering the personal investment when working professionally with families who are of the same race but are possibly from a different cultural background. In addition, I want to highlight the pressure one feels (whether perceived or real) when one is viewed by the dominant culture as the "cultural expert" (i.e. to know what is in the best interests for "one-of-your-own").

As can be seen, unwittingly, the situation is already set up with high expectations of the worker to be in the best position to help the client (in this case, family).[1] This is mostly because, *prima facie*, both worker and client share the same race, which seems to override the subtleties of culture and ethnicity. Hence, the worker is already slipping into a framework in which she may have difficulty re-configuring. By taking this formula for granted, the worker then becomes part of an equation in which she feels she has no choice but to use empathy as a therapeutic tool to aid her in trying to achieve what is in the best interests of the family. This is based on the assumption that due to their similar race, the worker and the client will also share understanding and, more pertinent to the therapeutic outcome (however this is defined), similar goals. Starting from this premise, it is difficult for the worker to step outside this set up and to question it without making herself

---

[1] "Worker" in this context refers to any professional (e.g. social worker, key worker, psychologist, therapist, counsellor, family therapist) who works in some type of therapeutic way with clients/families. For this chapter the terms "client" and "family" are used interchangeably.

susceptible to questioning her own professional abilities. She may also be struggling with the notion that she may let the family down. This is not just any family: it is a family in need from her "own community".

It then becomes obvious to the worker that maybe she was not selected solely on the basis of her professional qualifications, though these were essential, and that she was primarily chosen on the basis of her visible features—namely, her race—which had nothing to do with professional competence. The worker realizes that although she was appointed due to the combination of both these characteristics, paradoxically she will have to work doubly hard to demonstrate an emphasis on the application of the professional aspect. But with the knowledge that she was chosen for these two distinct aspects of the "person specification", the worker feels she can only give value for money by using both of these attributes (a kind of "two for the price of one" deal).

With the post comes the longed-for opportunity and challenge to demonstrate that one can do a good job. Such pressure heightens the worker's awareness that, if translated, "doing a good job" does not necessarily mean the best one can, but usually *more* than "*just* one's best". Similarly, with this awareness also comes the realization for the worker of the high expectations from her employer and the family, and she begins to feel that "all eyes are on her". Some researchers state that in many cases, but significantly less so for those of the dominant culture, race is both a political and a *personal* issue for ethnic-minority people (and professionals are no exception) (Banks, 1999; Helms & Carter, 1991; Thomas, 1995a).

Hence, there now comes into play a complicated and almost tautological balancing act. The worker has to learn to minimize the personal qualities that contributed to her selection (i.e. similarity of race) and, instead, put her professional skills as the uppermost attributes. However, this is done with the knowledge of the paradox that her professionalism is expected to be informed by this personal quality which she is trying to minimize in the first place, so that she can be perceived to be professionally competent.[2]

---

[2] This argument is not meant to dismiss the importance of equal opportunities and affirmative selection/recruitment of appropriately qualified ethnic-minority professionals in areas where they are underrepresented and their

With this framework, the worker becomes acutely aware that she now has to justify her selection by working extra hard in the best interest of the disadvantaged ethnic-minority clients. She has to uphold herself professionally and also work with the client using the personal "bonding" characteristic of race as one of the channels for communication in order to help the family. Interestingly, it may be that neither the family nor the worker ever mentions the issue of race, but its significance, though unspoken, may be understood to be a feature of their working relationship. In this context, "race" becomes a relationship enhancement.[3]

Case study

The setting

The setting is a residential unit for vulnerable families—that is, single mothers and their children. The unit is situated in one of the most deprived inner cities area in the south of England. The unit has many components of a therapeutic community, including weekly therapy for mothers and their children. The

---

presence would be of benefit for families/clients of similar ethnicity or culture. This is accepted as essential and relevant. However, the argument is the author's own personal debate. I wish to highlight the paradoxes that can occur when ethnic-minority professionals are selected due to their racial background and neither the worker nor the organisation has had many opportunities to get a sense of what it means for the family to be presented with a racially similar, but possibly culturally dissimilar, worker as the best offer available.

It can sometimes appear as if the goal was "recruit an ethnic-minority worker and then we will think of what to do next". There needs to be consideration beyond the appointment stage, such as relevant dynamics and possible strategies that revise current policies and procedures.

[3] A converse situation can occur when ethnic-minority workers work with ethnic-minority families or clients. Psychologists and researchers are aware that some ethnic-minority clients may not welcome the opportunity to work with a worker of the same ethnicity as them (d'Ardenne & Mahtani, 1999; Sue & Sue, 1999) and may view them with suspicion and mistrust (Cross, 1995; Helms & Carter, 1991), perceiving them to be "an enemy in the camp", a "sellout", a "traitor" who has been placed to "sell them out" and will do so (Carter, 1997).

dominant orientation of the therapeutic staff is psychodynamic.

Other components include weekly group/house meetings that include training and discussion around issues related to parenting. Violation of the unit's rules can result in warnings or instant dismissal.

The family

The family in Britain, residing in the unit, consists of a three-month-pregnant mother, "Soszie" (28 years old), son "Abdul" (6 years old), and daughter "Dina" (4 years old). The family is from East Africa and is seeking political asylum in Britain. They managed to escape persecution and the civil war, though they left behind the children's father (Soszie's husband) and their entire extended network. Since their arrival in Britain, two months earlier, the family have resided in the residential unit. At the time of their arrival Soszie was not aware that she was pregnant, and she was expecting her husband to join the family in Britain within a few weeks. The last time the family heard from Soszie's husband or any extended family members was just before they left East Africa to settle in Britain. The family were placed in the unit by social services because of concerns over Abdul's "out of control behaviour". There have also been concerns about his inappropriate sexualized behaviour. The purpose of the residential placement was to assess the family and to provide them with a degree of independence prior to being rehoused.

The issue of focus

One Friday evening, an argument between Abdul and another resident, an Asian boy named "Dipak" (8 years old) escalated into a physical fight. Dipak seemed to have suffered worse than Abdul and immediately went crying to his mother, showing her his bruises. Apparently, Abdul also returned to his flat but did not mention the fight to his mother. According to Soszie, Dipak's mother ("Nimesha") had been giving her aggressive "looks" and "stares" and also making confrontational gestures such as poking her tongue out and using finger signs to Soszie the whole weekend but had not said anything to her. On the Sunday evening, Soszie was descending the stairs to go out. As she reached the bottom of the stairs, she became very distressed at the sight and sound of her son in tears as Nimesha, in her broken English, screamed and shouted abuse, including racist remarks, at him. Enraged by this scene, she physically attacked Nimesha. Nimesha did not retaliate. Instead, she straightaway presented herself to the duty office, in a dishevelled state with a scarred face and chunks of her hair missing from her scalp, to report the incident. This was recorded and both families were told that this matter would be discussed with the whole team, who would then decide the outcome.

The dilemma

- Should both families be removed from the unit even though only one of them has committed a breach (of violence) that has as its penalty instant termination of residency?
- Should the black worker empathize with the family in her care and suggest that Soszie had been subjected to enduring psychological taunts over the weekend and had reacted as a mother to protect her young? If the black worker uses this as an argument for re-evaluation of the instant-eviction policy, would she run the risk of, at the very least, being perceived by her white colleagues as overidentifying with this black family? Would this be calling her professionalism into question?
- Would a worker of either culture (African or Asian) be "the best referee", in this case, of what should happen to the families? And, if so, how would she or he work creatively cross-culturally?
- Would the best decision be made by workers who are not from either of the families' cultures, on the assumption that they are more likely to be neutral (i.e. that they would make less of a biased decision when utilizing professional objec-

tivity than possibly one made by one of the ethnic-minority workers representing each of the families?[4]

- Do the different ways in which the two families dealt with the issue represent distinct cultural differences, and, if so, should such cultural patterns of relating be taken into account? What exactly does it mean to take "culture" into account?

The above case illustrates a difficulty in working with vulnerable families when hierarchical structures/boundaries are blurred to the extent that the adult parents from different families take the "role" of their individual children and become focused on what was originally their children's issues. This is a typical example and one that many family therapists and those working with families (e.g. teachers, educational or child psychologists) probably see regularly. However, this case is chosen to illustrate how the situation can become even more complicated when issues of culture and ethnicity are involved. In many situations, the cases that one comes across may involve disputes between families where, commonly, one of the families is from the dominant culture. Similarly, it may be that the family is from an ethnic-minority community and the worker is from the host community, giving the impression that issues are "black and white", clear-cut. Indeed, training courses, manuals, and other materials have now become profi-

---

[4] It could be mistakenly inferred from this dilemma that the author is suggesting that ethnic-minority workers have a vulnerability to become attached to and overidentify with their ethnic-minority clients, making it difficult for them to work professionally and deal objectively with issues as they arise. The author is not stating this. The point is that, equipped with the additional knowledge of another cultural perspective, such workers may be in a position to provide a different type of explanation compared to the usual Western understandings of behaviour. It is conceivable that the workers may be attached to their own cultural mores, and in some way, even unconsciously, in such an instance may feel called to defend them. This can unwittingly lead to the presentation of both cases being overshadowed by a "battle of cultures". Such insights into the families' context from at least two other cultural perspectives may make it difficult to decide what should be the outcome since in many cases neither way is right or wrong—just different. It is, of course, understood that in our society emotional cruelty to children and violence against adults in most incidences are unacceptable.

cient at developing an awareness in alerting family and individual workers/therapists to recognizing when oppression or discrimination is taking place. Although, as therapists, we are still trying to grapple with this task of acting fairly, the complications increase when both "injured" families are from ethnic-minority cultures. The assumption seems to be that the worker will be able to understand, communicate, and probably represent ethnic-minority families from this background. However, the worker is then continually reminded to assess the family using dominant Western standards that also constitute the code of ethics to which his or her profession subscribe. This could create a potential trap for conflictual—or, at the very least, dual—roles.

The author's perspective

As a worker and counsellor in the residential unit, my argument was that while what Soszie did was wrong if we judged it as an act in isolation, it was not totally unreasonable if we considered it within the context of an instinctual reaction to provocation. Among the areas in which we assess families are the mother's parenting skills. I was aware that violence seemed to be a pattern of dealing with confrontational issues, and Soszie's violent retaliation to Nimesha seemed to reinforce Abdul's behaviour of resolving disputes by means of violence. In contrast, Nimesha's use of verbal abuse, such as insults and derision, appeared to exemplify to Dipak a general rule that the way to tackle challenging situations was to apply verbal provocation, such as ridicule, mockery, and scoffing. This would then be followed by attempts to get those in positions of power to collude with them as the "victim".

There were many issues to be considered in this case—not least the psychological effects of moving to a new culture ("cultural shock": Furnham & Bocher, 1988). Families in this position may also lack knowledge of the host's cultural attitudes towards the helping process. Such attitudes require disputes to be referred to those in formal and professional helping roles rather than resolving disputes on their own. Also, their different modes of communication would influence the way in which the family accesses and collaborates with the worker.

However, due to space constraints and for illustration, I would like to focus on one controversial issue that is complicated by stereotypes of different cultures. It is an issue that is not exclusive to residential units (though in this case the unit has provided the context) but transcends this context to the wider arena of working with families per se in any context.[5]

The issue centres on the use of violence both within and across families. My main concern was that if the East African family were evicted because of their violent responses to extreme provocation, they might be denied the opportunity as a family to explore the issues of violence, including any cultural contexts if relevant. There was the need to consider the message that we as professionals were giving to vulnerable families about using methods of provocation and violence as reactions at the intuitive level to challenging situations.

I had suggested that either both families were evicted or both families remained in the unit. The difficulty I had was in revealing that in my personal experience of black people and of working professionally with black clients and black families, I was aware that many, though not all, resorted to physical means as a way of disciplining their children and resolving adult disputes. However, while I was aware of this, I was also clear that this way of disciplining children was *not* emic (culture-specific). Yet in some cases such behaviours had been perceived as culturally bound and stereotypical. For Soszie, with regards to child-rearing practices this strategy was not interpreted as unacceptable or undue violence, mistreatment, or abuse, but a natural way to guide and train her children. In fact, many ethnic-minority members have been appalled by what they saw as emotional cruelty and psychological torment of typical Western forms of correction, such as rejection of children by acts such as ostracism (e.g. banishing children to their rooms), or restricting their freedom (e.g. "grounding" them). For many black families, short, sharp, shock treatments were pre-

---

[5] There are, of course, other pertinent issues in this case study—for example, the whole gambit/gallery of the Asian family's situation. There is no intention to minimize or ignore their experiences or perceptions, but this is not the focus of this chapter, and, as emphasized above, the case is for illustration purposes.

ferred in which punishment was not prolonged and children could learn, and hence benefit, from immediate feedback and soon afterwards return to being the object of their parents' affection. This was done as a way to signal that the acts of discipline were done within the context of loving parents who did not want to spare the rod and spoil the child, but wanted to fulfil their obligation of guiding their children along the right path.

The difficulty for me was that in presenting this point of view, and also being part of the black race, I ran the risk of being seen as holding those views.[6] I was acutely aware that I was training in a profession, and working in an environment, that holds as paramount the unacceptability of using physical means to discipline children. And indeed, these were potential child-protection issues. Therefore, it could be interpreted that, as a *perceived* advocate of such child-rearing practices, I held potentially a damaging—and hence unprofessional—perspective. It would not matter what model/paradigm I *actually* held. Indeed, it is more than likely that this would never be asked.

As a corollary, since I perceived myself to be acting in a professional manner, which included presenting another viewpoint in a way that I thought invited curiosity, it would not occur to me to make my own views on this explicit. After all, for me the professional issue was how accurately I could get across the family's views so that these could be understood within their cultural context and to represent these views clearly and fairly. It was also about how I could help the family work with the mismatch between their cultural views and the laws of the host culture. This is what I believed was an important part of my training and what I had been employed to do.

However, the other side of this is that I did have strong personal views about what should happen to this family. Because of the politics surrounding the sensitivity of dealing with ethnic-

---

[6] When families are discussed among workers, a shorthand way of identifying them is to refer to them as "*your* family" to the worker involved in their care. Although a common form of notation, "your family" somehow seems to take on a significant meaning when used in conversation with an ethnic-minority worker who has a similar ethnicity to the client family with whom she or he is working.

minority people in general, and even more so in professional settings, there seemed to be an atmosphere of discouragement in which to explore and deal with gut-level reactions towards the family. This unspoken, but very effective, suppression gave me the impression that I had to be very careful and would need to support my views with extensive "evidence". I could imagine how such a situation could make workers wary about disclosing strong feelings.

In relation to the conference

I felt that the above issues were very relevant to the focus of the IFT conference: to challenge and explore alternatives in anti-oppressive practices when working with clients and families from ethnic-minority backgrounds. The conference title was and is about dealing with issues around race and culture that, because of their sensitive nature, are potential minefields for getting it wrong. So, usually issues that should be discussed in the open are steered away from since a lot is at stake, not least one's professional integrity. For instance, at the conference Gill Gorell Barnes spoke about the experiences of being white, the lack of discussion about white identity, and hence the denial of opportunities to explore the usually presumptuous role of the powerful, dominant, mighty, majority culture. It was a kind of *fait accompli*: "whiteness" brought with it the automatic assumption to that position. These very important issues about race can contribute to the progress of practice, but in many cases they are left unsaid because of the risks involved in exposing one's self when bringing them out into the open and discussing them. The proverbial feeling seems to be that some things are better left unsaid.

But in order to combat oppressive practices, it is important to work as a cross-cultural team. Hence, some things are not better left unsaid. Writers in the field of family therapy (e.g. Boyd-Franklin, 1989) and therapy in general (Pedersen, 1997) have spoken of the concept of "cultural brokers". A therapist working with a family whose culture she or he is not familiar with could either team up with a worker of that family's country of origin or approach another worker knowledgeable about that culture (the cultural broker) for advice. It is, however, important to recognize that practitioners not of the family's culture can engage with ethnic-minority families and individuals (Richards, 2000). In fact, in some cases, ethnic-minority workers may be received with more suspicion from client families who share the same culture (Carter, 1997).

This means that as part of a multicultural team, experiences and knowledge need to be shared, but this may involve taking some risks. It seems that many working in the field of family and individual therapy have acknowledged that risk-taking and playing it safe are actually part of the same continuum. In order to take risks so that therapists can work creatively with clients, the atmosphere of discouragement referred to above needs to be replaced by a safe-enough environment in which they feel they can explore their dilemmas and the risks that evolve from them (Mason, 1993; Byng-Hall, 1995). A similar conclusion emerged from interview data of workers at a general family-counselling agency presented in Rossiter, Walsh-Bowers, and Prilleltensky's (1996) qualitative research paper, "Learning from Broken Rules". So, from this it would seem that to be able to work creatively workers need to be able to have a dialogue about dilemmas. In some cases, these dilemmas may be seen as ethical dilemmas. Hence, such dialogue demands a high level of risk-taking that can feel unsafe in the organization. Some measures need to be developed that would produce the required safe space for open dialogue among team members.

The workshop

Of course, before that safe space can be cultivated, the needs and vulnerabilities of workers should to be taken into account. My own experiences led me to conclude that the conference needed a workshop that helped participants appreciate what it feels like to be the "racial other" (Jung, 1930). Since the majority of those attending the conference were of the dominant culture, "the racial other" would be those from an ethnic-minority background.

My intention was to get participants to assume a racially different role, so that they would begin to get a sense of the different forms of dilemmas and hence the various levels of perceptions of what could be at stake for the worker when speaking out on race-related issues. White workers would have the opportunity to explore what it is like to feel strongly about an issue as an ethnic-minority person, yet to be aware of the need to think carefully before a decision is made to disclose such emotions because of the likely potential consequences and preconceived ideas of the listener(s). Similarly, it may help them to appreciate the restrictions on behaviour and articulating certain types of viewpoints or proposals. These are developed within a context of not wanting to fulfil stereotypes of ethnic minorities being too sensitive or of making decisions based almost exclusively on emotion and feelings of injustice.

For the ethnic-minority worker in the role of a white person, there would be the opportunity to assume membership of the dominant culture. This could include not feeling the need to reflect on one's racial identity so much, to consider what this meant in terms of perceptions of egalitarianism, with everyone having the same level of autonomy, and hence that risk-taking had the same (perceived) consequences for everyone, regardless of race. Such perceptions and assumptions would have an impact on cross-racial dynamics when working with ethnic-minority colleagues and also ethnic-minority families.

The exercise

The exercise was done in pairs, with one participant taking on the role of a client family member and the other participant taking on the role of a worker. This involved participants getting into role of one particular family member from one of the families with whom they had worked transracially or cross-culturally. The "family member" would tell the other participant, the "worker", a little about her/himself. This usually included race and cultural background, age, gender, family composition, presenting problem, and context of referral. With this information, the "worker" would assume some characteristics that were different, at least in some cultural way, from those of the family member. He or she would then start working on the problem with the family member. The family member would then verbally make explicit those interventions that she or he considered ran the risk of being cultural *faux pas* or stereotypes or demonstrated a certain level of cultural competency. The next part of the task was for the family member to consider whether these interventions would reduce or increase the distance that initially existed between her or his family and the worker. Concurrently, the worker would openly disclose the dilemmas she or he perceived and the level of risk involved depending on the intervention or decision she or he made.

Issues from the workshop

For the participants, this was a challenging and exhausting but stimulating exercise. In many ways it was also frustrating because of the initial difficulties in conceptualizing being in a very different and for many, an inconceivable "role". This invited discussion about the extent to which it is possible to be truly empathic towards ethnically different families. This was especially so for those working with families from ethnic-minority communities who were unlikely to share the same cultural values as their worker, who was probably from the host culture. It was acknowledged that even though we all have time pressures when working with families, the overall time is longer than was available in the workshop and is usually sufficient to enable us to build up a relationship with them over time. Also, we have more opportunities "to try to put it right if we get it wrong".

One of the main dilemmas that arose from the workshop was how a worker balances the thin line between sometimes "bracketing" culturally held views and knowing when to bring them into play. This was an issue for both those working transracially and also those who shared similar racial and some cultural features with the families with whom they worked. In some instances, there was a concern that cultural aspects were not given enough significance when trying to understand families' patterns of behaviour and their way of making sense of what was happening to them. There was also the concern of falling into the trap of making generalizations and assumptions about certain cultures so that the worker unintentionally ran the risk of stereotyping the family on that basis (for example, people from ethnic-minority backgrounds are "emotional" and because of this have a tendency to make irrational decisions; e.g. see Sue & Sue, 1999). This seemed to be especially the case for workers who were not from the same culture as the ethnic-minority family. There was also the acknowledgement that preconceived ideas could also come into play when ethnic-minority workers work with such families. In some cases, this led to conflicting feelings of, on the one hand, needing to safeguard ethnic-minority families yet, on the other, feeling exposed and embarrassed by some of the families' practices.

The multiple complexities inherent in the practice of individual and family therapy were evident along with the difficulties in choosing between dilemmas. Hence, it could be argued that in some cases non-discriminatory practices for professionals sometimes do not take account of the needs of the family, especially if their needs or worldviews are different. It appeared that for ethnic-minority workers working with ethnic-minority families, there was the possibility of families wanting to include the worker as "one of us". This pull posed the danger of dual relationships and a potential conflict of interest. One way to deal with this struggle is to seek the opinion of a "level-headed mentor". Another possible strategy is, when presenting difficulties due to contradictory choices in supervision, to couch them in such a way that demonstrates awareness of the worker's responsibility for maintenance of professional standards. As can be seen, these are two different strategies with probably different outcomes. The point seemed to be that when working with ethnic-minority families, depending on whom one was approaching, the worker needed to be vigilant and aware of the impact of the way in which she or he presented her or his perception of the case. This applies to workers from all cultures. (And, in retrospect, could be applied to work with all clients regardless of race.)

It was highlighted that risk-taking should also be interpreted as a proactive and responsible act. Such a strategy should not always be seen as an unwitting act or even a dilemma but as taken because a healthy need for change had been noticed. There is also the probability that perhaps some professionals are more likely to take risks than are other professionals. I think that trainees, especially early on in their career, are less likely to take risks than are fully qualified and more experienced therapists/workers.

One participant, as a "black family member", spoke about the feelings of helplessness, almost being stripped of all her power and autonomy, and the desperation to hold on to some feelings of dignity. She spoke about becoming even more entrenched in cultural traditions as a way to empower herself and her family. She was aware that this would distance her from her "white" worker. This seemed to indicate the need for a mechanism whereby clients could candidly disclose their discomfort over sharing certain secrets and practices with culturally different workers without feeling that they would be penalized for taking this risk (subject to, for example, competent child-protection practice).

Another participant stated that one of the most risky things for her was to actually be open about what she really thought and felt, for fear of making a mistake. However, she said she realized that by not testing her hypotheses she ran the risk of becoming "culturally encapsulated" (Pedersen, 1997) since the result could be that she would never expose her ideas. Hence, she would deny herself the opportunity to learn and to grow.

Conclusions

This chapter has explored sensitive issues that pose risks and dilemmas when working cross-culturally and when the merging of personal and professional issues occur. For instance, the potential quandary of race-matching (but not necessarily cultural-matching) of families and workers from ethnic-minority communities.

One of the main (unspoken) reasons why many black workers are selected for some positions among many other candidates is probably because they are from an ethnic-minority group that is underrepresented professionally but overrepresented in client groups. When one considers this, it will not be surprising that they are likely to have many same-race families allocated to them.

Although they may not be the perfect cultural match for all these families, they may be the "best" that can be offered to the families. It is acknowledged that ethnic-minority workers should be available for such families; however, how it works in practice has not been thoroughly discussed and communicated, and so difficulties can arise when this opportunity reaches fruition or realization.

The controversial issue of violence was used as an example of the dilemmas that the ethnic-minority worker faces when trying to put across a view of a family from the same race as hers. By presenting a different cultural perspective in a convincing manner, the worker ran the risk of being associated with that view, even if this assumption was never made explicit by her colleagues, who may then jump to the conclusion that her professionalism should be queried. With the type of work considered here—that is, therapy—there is more vulnerability to feel very strongly about certain situations or outcomes in relation to clients. Workers get to know "their families" well, hence making them more likely to understand and even champion their worldviews. This can potentially happen to any worker, regardless of race. However, for the ethnic-minority worker, there is the added dimension of race and the possibility that when she or he is presenting an ethnic-minority family's perspective she or he may also, though not always, adhere to it. This can cause difficulties if it is different from the dominant view in the profession. In fact, in some cases professional and personal issues can become so entwined that it is difficult to separate them without feeling that some essential ingredient has been lost.

Hence it seems to me that one of the growth areas during training is in developing the ego strength necessary to feel, as a professional from an ethnic-minority background, that it is acceptable to convincingly present a viewpoint that is from clients who share one's "community". By doing so, one is using one's cultural knowledge to help one act professionally and ensure that those clients and families whose worldviews differ from the norm are treated in an ethical and responsive manner (Lee, 1991). This can only be done if professionals involved have sufficient information about cultural variations before they make important decisions.

Corey, Schneider-Corey, and Callanan (1992) state that "Professionals must ultimately struggle with the issues of responsible practice", and this is to do with professional issues that mostly affect the actual *practice* of therapy. It seems relevant to acknowledge that by learning and constantly revisiting professional issues around working with ethnic-minority families, we are not only witnessing our professional development, but are also in a continuous process of personal development. This would seem particularly so when working with difference in the therapeutic relationship, such as clients and families from different ethnic backgrounds. From the professional aspect, we are careful to make sure that each client is treated equally within the legal and professional codes, and that no client is discriminated against because of such individual difference as race, gender, ethnicity, culture, religion, and disability.

This seems all above-board and politically correct. But dissonance can occur when working with some families. For instance, the "personal" side may strongly believe on moral grounds that, for this family, paradoxically some type of discrimination needs to take place. This may be necessary for the family to truly benefit, as equally as any other family, from the services available. That is, the client needs to be treated differently in order for services to have the same impact that they have in helping other families.

Working creatively to deal with the said and done

From my own personal experiences and what I have gained from the workshop and the conference as a whole, I have learned that there are many workers who are indeed frequently dealing creatively with their struggles and conflicts when working with ethnic-minority families (Sawyerr, 1999). Contributors to this book provide an immediate example, but there are many more. Different perceptions of risk and risk-taking may mean that what one member of staff sees as risk-taking, another worker may perceive as working within the professional guidelines. Hence, it is acknowledged that there will always be colleagues who do not share one's perspective, because they have different approaches to risk-taking. This could mean that in some instances it becomes more of a value judgement than a technical judgement as to whether a risk has been taken.

There are suggestions around in the literature that aim to help family therapists reduce their vulnerability to taking risks that are seen to violate practical standards—for example, Brock's "At Risk Test for Marriage and Family Therapists" (1997). However, I find the steps from Neihart's "Systematic Risk-taking" (1999) useful as a strategy to help us as therapists develop our skills and increase our self-esteem and confidence in taking risks when working with ethnic-minority families, especially when working cross-culturally. They are:

- understanding the benefits;
- initial self-assessment/assessment of family's situation;
- identifying needs of family and one's own professional integrity;
- determining a risk to take;
- taking the risk;
- processing the experience.

I think that once we can fully process the experience, then we can learn from it. It is only then that we can begin to make more informed choices about the consequences of taking the risk. However, the essence of dilemmas is that we do not always know the impact of taking a risk, and it may be these challenges that keep our personal enthusiasm and investment in our profession alive.

Of course, in order to maintain and harness our personal enthusiasm we have to be attentive to this source of energy. For me, it comes in the form of my brother Desmond, my mother Lyra, and my father David who have grounded me in my identity, and continue to do so, and whose love, support, and encouragement have helped me reach "where I'm at", both personally and professionally.

Acknowledgements. Special thanks to Alice Sawyerr for her exchange of ideas regarding personal and professional, issues related to this chapter. I would like to thank Aubrey Baillie and Professor Helen Cowie, both at the University of Surrey Roehampton, for their comments on earlier drafts of this chapter.

PART IV

PERSONAL AND PROFESSIONAL DEVELOPMENT PERSPECTIVES

CHAPTER 9

Getting it right, getting it wrong: developing an internal discourse about ethnicity and difference

Gill Gorell Barnes

A subject like this deserves a book from each one of us, rather than a chapter. I have been asked to contribute a personal chapter but this is part of a more extended exploration about difference and culture to which I return with different questions at different times. I shall focus here on selected aspects of my early family experience. I see this as contributing to my developing awareness that in order to respect and value ethnic differences between people, a context has to exist in which differences themselves, rather than conformity, can be acknowledged as of value. I have thought about "getting it right and getting it wrong" at the earliest stages in my life, both in relation to external conversations about "others who are different" as well as to internalized racist discourses, conversations held in the family when I was a child and dwelling therefore somewhere in my mind as I grew up, although not necessarily held in my conscious mind.

The time bites I have included here include times when conformity was the paramount value in the immediate context I was in: my pre-adolescent life with my family and friends, pre-political consciousness; working in another culture in the United States in the early 1960s, which was the proper dawn and development of conscious awareness of ethnicity as a political issue; the daily consciousness that difference also means disagreement; working alongside African-Caribbean men and women, from the 1960s (Arnold, 1974; Gorell Barnes, 1975) to the present day. Thinking about gender and power in the 1980s and developing antiracist-practice conferences in the 1990s are referred to and referenced but not discussed. The chapter also leaves out any detailed personal recounting of my experience of the English class system and the political influences of the men I lived with as a child and a young adult; from Fabian socialist father to Thatcher-supporter stepfather and husband. Such major influences and their impact are germane, but need another context for exploration.

In writing about "ethnicity" at all, one of the traps for white Anglo-Saxon English people has been to think first about other, rather than self. A quotation from Sandra Harding, drawn to my attention in 1996 by my daughter, summarizes the change that thinking about gendered issues with my colleagues and friends from the 1980s onwards signalled for me also in relation to ethnicity: "[A feminist point of enquiry] which joins other underclass approaches in insisting on the importance of studying ourselves and 'studying up' rather than 'studying down'" (Harding, 1987, p. 6) has become a central feature of the way I address issues in private and in public. When I was trained as a "psychiatric social worker" the inclusion of the self in thinking about "society" was explicitly discouraged as "subjective" and therefore of lesser value. We were encouraged to be "objective" and speak as though we could distance ourselves from the social phenomena we described.

Throughout all our lives there are likely to be tensions between received attitudes and our own experience. Socially constructed aspects of the self, which include definitions of gender and ethnicity that have been imprinted on us at different stages of our own development, as children and within families and intimate relationships (Gorell Barnes, 1995), will become inner constructions about self and others which constantly have to be re-examined in the context of different encounters in our everyday personal and professional lives. This is a life-long job.

While working on this chapter I read in a family assessment, written by an experienced fully trained (English white Caucasian) social worker, the statement: "There are racial issues here, the baby's father being Greek." This gave me a small piece of external confirmation that the half-truths and whispers I am describing here as some of the more intangible nuances of racist thinking continue to have validity over time. They do not only belong to the earlier era of my childhood, with which I open up the story of becoming aware of ethnicities as "difference" in a postwar "modernist" Britain.

Early childhood: north-west London 1945–1955

The initial "difference" I describe is that my mother came from a culture that Boots the chemist defined in a New-Millennium hair range, "Mediterranean". This was poised uneasily, in my family's case, somewhere between Western Europe, North Africa, and Western Asia and flanked by countries with fiercely divided religious affiliations: Catholic, Muslim, and Orthodox Christian. The first "difference" is now defined by me as having a family who I could see lived and behaved differently from the norms and perspectives of middle-class white English people (that being the overarching system of values within which I grew up in the 1950s) while at the same time encouraging me to aspire to values to which they paid only lip service.

North-west London in the 1940s and the 1950s was populated by a superficially homogeneous ethnicity, "white Caucasian". This was itself a highly complex series of "yoked" subsystems distinguished by class, ethnicity of origin, and first nationality loosely rooted into a notional consensus of aspiring to the values of an Anglo-Saxon, upper-middle-class group. This in turn apparently modelled itself on patterns of behaviour thought to show affinity to those connected to the nobility of England, and to royalty and their hierarchically arranged kin, whose affiliation to godliness, through closeness to royalty, scaffolded public notions of "correctness" and "moral values". The superior worth attributed to royalty and nobility had publicly acclaimed validity, not only through the Church of England and its prayers for the Royal Family, but also through other popular national institutional voices like the BBC and the press. The national anthem was played at the beginning and end of films, at the theatre, and even at the circus. At the level of "coherence of beliefs", perceived through the eyes of a 7-year-old, the structures of society were still closely organized by the recent major world war, in which, as a result of the large-scale bombing of the civilian population and the parallel discoveries of poverty, filth, and ill-health in the large cities, many previously divided sections of society had been temporarily shaken closer together. Loyalty to King and Queen had been reinforced by the then Queen's commitment to staying in London throughout the blitz, Buckingham Palace itself receiving a direct hit. Class structures in the cities at least had been intersected and temporarily disorganized by the destruction and new structures of war, and when urban society tried to reorder itself it was clear that things could never be the same again. The profound differences this would lead to, in terms of different thinking within different parts of Britain, had not yet been envisaged. The major foundations of the Welfare State, the health service, and the reorganized education system had been laid down by the time that I was 4 years old, and the systems of welfare-benefits-for-all were made law before I went to school. People wanted a fairer society, and many people who were later to vote for Margaret Thatcher voted for a Labour government at that time.

I was a child of the Welfare State, made conscious of it by my Fabian socialist father and proud of it. Indeed, it was the reason I drank my foul cod-liver oil everyday, because the state had provided it for me to make me big and strong. Childhood, however, despite the apparent homogeneities of skin colour, health, education, and welfare for all, was awash with undefined subtleties of "difference", the "them" and the "us" that seemed so hard to pin down. It was so important apparently, at times, to my mother, so scoffed at by my father, and so frightening if I, as a child, got them—whatever they were—wrong.

What indeed were "us" in terms of social positioning? I was the first English—and, as it turned out, only—child of my generation born to either side of my family, English and Greek, in this country. The Greek side of the family had migrated into Britain after the First World War, my grandfather making a lot of money as an "engineer entrepreneur" and then losing all of it in the Depression of the 1930s. My mother went out to earn from the age of 17, after a Catholic convent education. This was the closest religion to Greek Orthodoxy offering an education that her parents could find, Orthodoxy being the faith in which my grandmother remained devout until her death when I was 33. My mother was always the primary breadwinner in my childhood, my father being more interested in ideologies than making money. Although neither parent had achieved higher education, or had been deprived of it by family misfortune, family expectations of my own education were both extremely high and also, on my mother's side, highly ambivalent. My Greek aunt once sent me a letter with a disguised warning about growing away from your family through too much education. As I was the only child in the family to enter university in either country, this message carried some weight.

Belonging to two cultures can give you more than one lens through which to examine issues of ethnicity, if circumstances allow you to make the differences conscious and reflect what they mean to you. Each ethnicity will bring its own "singularities" to bear on family life. However, achieving a position from which to think is not easy as a child, particularly if you are an "only". The extent of my "Greekness" as "difference" in postwar British society has become clearer to me only in the last twenty years, as issues of gender and ethnicity have taken on a high priority in my daily working and thinking life. What Margaret Mead referred to as the scientific evidence of the senses initially saturated me with knowledge of my own difference, the culture soaked up through the senses at a very early age. My early experience of religious belief in itself exposed me to a plurality of sensuous rituals, sprinkled as I was with Holy Water, anointed with oil in front of the icons with the burning candles at festivals, and stuffed with holy bread (stale and tasteless) all by my Greek grandmother, mocked by my agnostic sceptical English father, and secretly smuggled into Catholic churches to light candles of atonement or "special pleading" by my mother in case my grandmother (and the nuns by whom she herself was educated) were right and I was going to be damned after all for not having been baptized—one issue in which it seems my father triumphed (until the Church of England claimed me with my marriage at the age of 22). It was only long after my grandmother's death that the fears underlying her actions became clearer to me as my mother, having survived the deaths of two husbands, rejoined the Catholic faith she had put aside in the face of the scorn of the two Englishmen she had married. I understood that in all those holy gestures my Greek grandmother (female) had taken upon herself the role of priest (male), ensuring me a regular supply of the representations of the body and blood of Christ (male) to safeguard against the devil (male) stealing away my (female) unbaptized soul. No wonder sex was a dangerous subject in the family, never in my memory, discussed but only alluded to as something "dangerous" and associated with the "east".

Gender

Child development theory has taught that gender is a powerful organizer of social functioning in children. Once a child understands the categories of gender, she or he is likely to use this influential classification to organize the way she or he sees and understands family and close social events (Haste, 1987; Lloyd, 1987; Maccoby, 1980). Gender schema—concepts organizing definitions of what belongs to male and female behaviour—and constructs of social-role relationships such as mother/daughter, wife/husband, son/father, son/mother, and so forth are said to be extremely resistant to change and disconfirmation after the third year of childhood. Thus a child in a family where roles are clearly defined and allocated and agreed will, it is asserted, form impressions that gendered arrangements operate along clearly demarcated lines. However, a child such as myself—who had two grandmothers who cooked, but a mother who refused to cook; a father who cooked both at home and at work, and a mother who often left for work before I got up and returned after I was in bed; an uncle who lay around at home writing books on philosophy and astronomy while his sister supported him financially and his mother waited on him hand and foot (literally not metaphorically)—grows up with a number of mixed messages about gender and role which are likely to lead her to question and explore arrangements rather than make assumptions about how they operate (for other discussions, see Ochs & Taylor, 1992; Steadman, 1985). Such questioning is also likely to develop in relation to other forms of received wisdom, such as opinions about others, based on ethnic stereotyping. As with all cultures, there were often contradictory and conflicting messages operating simultaneously. My mother's family "spoke" thus. "Become English, but don't be disloyal by forgetting you are Greek." I think that one of the contradictions at the highest level was: "Marry a good [English]) man but don't ever do anything a 'husband' [man] tells you because [Greek] women basically run things"—a message deeply embedded in Greek culture but hidden within the "inside home/outside home" scenarios. Also, "Never rely on any man for income"—a message developed perhaps by two generations of "failed businessmen" (but also based on the idea that men's job is to think and women's is to see that things work smoothly, interdependent with: "Even if we the Greek women have to pretend to be dependent on our men for survival, we know its only a facade we put up for the smooth running of family life."

The message, then, was "Marry West not East" and, at some further level, was "The further east you go the more dangerous it gets." Issues of religious affiliation were more predominant than those of skin colour. Half-told stories of my grandmother being "kidnapped" for the white-slave trade in the Hanging Gardens of Babylon permeated my childhood mythology. Indeed, the white-slave trade was of more preoccupation to my grandmother than the black-slave trade, a subject never discussed. Life in the Greek household was marked by the presence of religion, the preoccupation with moralities of dubious and ill-defined forms, and the absence of a political and socially diverse world outside. Ethnic difference was denoted by religion more than by any other "marker"—Turks, Jews, and Arabs being the reference points in my grandmother's mind. There was no discussion about the Greek Civil War, only a later startling (to me) assumption that I would understand that a socialist prime minister was a bad thing because he might let the communists in and they had taken 30,000

Greek children to Albania to indoctrinate them in wrong thinking (and maybe turn them into Muslims) (see Safaris & Eve, 1990).

Friends

For a mind to develop as a child, it seems to me important that questions can be asked elsewhere about what is suppressed in family conversations. In the days before television, and with limited discussion on the radio, the importance of friends—a peer group that itself contains differences—could not be overemphasized, for an only child in particular. Thus my first socially constructed sensitization to awareness of "ethnicity" formed through scrutiny and discussion, rather than through the senses and the absence of discussion, came about in the many contexts of "Jewishness" in the postwar London milieu in which I lived for the first twelve years. My closest friends were from Jewish families, and the nuances of what made good or less "respectable" Jewish families was a matter of speculation, as attitudes from different parents came into the playground through their daughters for discussion and dissection. Issues of money, social standing acquired through wealth, the size of the flat you lived in, who had the first TV sets, whose parents had a car, or even two cars, and the key question "what job does your father do" kept me at a low level of unease since my parents seemed unplaceable in the structures available. They were neither of the "old" professions or aspirations, nor clearly part of new ones that anyone else recognized.

The third influence in my preadolescent life alongside family and friends was literature, or, to be more simple, "books". I read, continuously and voraciously, anything that came my way, including much that I did not understand and much that scared me. Spending much time on my own, I had read everything at home by the age of 9 years, including all of Bernard Shaw and the New Testament, much of the Old Testament, my mother's Edwardian children's encyclopaedias, and several years of "Book of the Month Club," before I learned how to use the local library and discovered a world of children's authors. The *Reader's Digest*, which my parents took, and *Picture Post*, which my English grandmother took, provided many horrific and detailed accounts of aspects of the war; heroic resistance fighters who had been captured, long descriptions of the tortures they had endured, and some of the earliest pictures of the concentration camps alongside the descriptions of what was found by those who had gone into them after the Germans had left. My father I now think wished me to know about evil, and so a book called *The Scourge of the Swastika* entered our household. I remember reading it on a number 74 bus on the route to my grandmother's, being aware, without having any political awareness, of some of the horrifying effects of racism in relation to people whom I saw as part of myself: my Jewish friends from school and their families. There was something common to these friends, which I could not see myself, that had led to another country classifying them as dangerous and a threat, and to be disposed of. Huge personal questions about what I would have done if my own friends were threatened in this way opened up before me, because I was somehow aware, without being clear why, that "they" would not have come for me. (Had I known more about the German occupation of Greece at that time, this view might well have been different; Mazower, 1993.)

1964: U.S. Homogeneity

I am now going to jump a decade: adolescence a blur of academic struggle, unfulfilled sexuality but gaining my street cred as a "both-sides-of-the-counter" daughter of a Soho coffee-bar owner, my father's resolution of the tension between intellect, cooking, and attempting to earn money. I move to a second time zone of "experiencing difference in relation to ethnicity" in a more conscious way. When I was 21, in 1964, I went to work in the United States—only for three months, but a proper break from the United Kingdom. Sponsored by an American youth organization I was placed with a radio and TV station in the Northwest, following a Greyhound-bus ride across the States which is an opening for hearing people's life stories as you travel. The educational part of the scheme involved staying with six different families selected to show me different facets of the U.S. way of life in a small town. I learnt to love country & western music, to go through the rituals of drive-in movies, to observe the qualifying rounds for the Miss

Northwest Washington State beauty pageant, and more bizarrely was taken to the John Birch Society which is a right-wing racist group concerned with—well, I'm not sure what, because a lot of ritual went on what appeared to have little relevance to anything I could discuss. However, there was that "swastika" again, flagged up in an unfamiliar context. Becoming aware that an active racist streak ran through this seemingly smooth-running rural area was heavily endorsed when I subsequently met and "dated" a black man and was called up in front of the station director and warned off any further contact, "for my own good". The extraordinary experience of being stone-walled in public in a "diner" by white people I knew well, because I was in the company of a black man, is a stark vignette I can remember today; it was one of the triggers to an unreflective anger that led me into a more vigorous curiosity about the Civil Rights movement, a student journalistic critiquing of the society I was visiting, and contributed subsequently to a decision to do an MSc in Social Policy and Mental Health at the London School of Economics. Studying "American" gave me a restlessness to "study English".

Internalized racist discourse

In thinking about "getting it right and getting it wrong", I want to reflect back to the dangers of internalized racist discourse as part of "family values". If we believe that stories about the self are never fixed but emerge in different forms in different contexts, this allows us the opportunity for new understanding and new discourse to evolve at any point in our lives, particularly within the context of changes offered by intimate relationships such as partners, friends, and growing children. Nonetheless, such evolution may also involve challenge of old systems of which any of us have been a part and therefore cause pain to intimate others and discomfort or possible misery to the self.

In any family that is trying to assimilate into a new country, there may be times at which critical comments about the family and its own values and attitudes about others can become unsafe. There is also the question of how disputes and conflicts inside the family in relation to its own acculturation are dissipated or minimized by uniting against "the other". The "other" can be anyone who is framed as less fortunate or more socially marginalized than "this family", the criteria for "otherness" often remaining bewildering to the children of the family long after they leave home. This "uniting of the family" at the expense of another group can become a habit, persisting long after any unifying function it may have originally served, and it may be used as shorthand for defining "them and us" long after an individual family member may choose not to be defined by the family group in such a way.

As a girl child in a Mediterranean family, the double expectation of conformity was that family "rules" would be maintained both inside the home and outside the home. Issues of loyalty and the taboo against debate, discussion, and above all disagreement can also underpin a culture of racism. Dealing with internalized racism is therefore, for any of us, also often dealing with the unchallenged voices of family in childhood. In many family cultures, like my own, issues of loyalty are specific not only to the nuclear family but to the larger kinship group. In a situation where the group is a minority ethnicity, to be loyal to family values at a time when that culture may see itself as under threat through migration (and in my family's case, through the additional dimension of a country torn apart by civil war) has multi-layered meanings. Where a group whose social and political discourse is marginalized and the individuals within it see the changing traditions in which their identity is in part bound up as in particular need of preservation, acknowledging the competing needs, values, and aspirations of other migrant groups as legitimate becomes subordinated to "valourizing" the values and aspirations of the host society as an easier way of preserving the semblance of "family coherence".

As Edward Said puts it in his autobiography, *Out of Place* (1999), his Egyptian father when challenged would say of America, his first-generation country of migration: "My country, right or wrong." So it was for my mother and "her" England, a country that probably stopped developing in her mind around about 1944 when she was at the peak of her career in the film studios of beleaguered, war-torn, but valiant and ultimately victorious Britain.

The gatekeepers to a new country or culture are often school-age children, holding the tension between the old culture and the new, perhaps the first to learn the language and assimilate host-country peer-group culture and recognize the tension it creates with the older people from the country of origin. My grandmother never learned good English; my mother never spoke good Greek, and I was prohibited from learning it, as a "useless" language. I was the second generation, the English generation, the first to go to an English school and learn the rules of London-born "others". My mother, I think, carried all the anxieties of the first generation, creating her own rules and trading on beauty, rather than correctness, to get herself to the "right" place in English society. She always wanted her daughter to know "what was correct", and, failing to allow for change in the society to whose hidden rules she still believed there was a key, she was always from my perspective a generation out of date.

In systemic therapy, attention is paid to the concept of "dominant and marginalised voices" (Gorell Barnes, 1998). These can be conceptualized as an inner dialogue belonging to childhood, but in my personal and professional experience such voices rarely come only from within the individual and belong to their past. They can also be found to be active and ongoing in the current family to which the individual remains connected, even when they are well grown. The racism that was there in the form of folk tales, or family stories, when you were a child is still likely to be there when you are an adult, and its expression is likely to seem more offensive and less anodyne. For me, it took the context of a second partnership and an awareness that I did not want *my* children growing up in the confused tangles of unacknowledged racist attitudes before I could openly challenge the covert racism that I had lived alongside all my childhood. Even as an adult, I could not have had an open confrontation—with all the connotations of disloyalty and ingratitude—without my partner and without the support of one of my oldest and best friends, both of them Jewish in their different ways. Each helped me to tackle in a family context the unacknowledged and denied family attitudes that should have been more openly confronted by me many years before (also see Cooklin & Gorell Barnes, 1994).

Deconstructing racism in the family and in the mind takes many forms. In my view, racism is multi-layered, multi-positioned, and liable to hit you from any angle when you least expect it. It has to be constantly confronted openly and plainly. Until you are able to move around yourself and the intimate contexts of home and relationships, workplace and relationships, and friendship, zapping these unexpected voices with an internal as well as an external laser, you remain at risk for getting it wrong rather than getting it right.

Hazards for professionals

What are likely to be the hazards, then, for professionals working with people of ethnicities different from their own if they have not thought about their own issues of gender, culture, and role in relation to the family structures and variations of others. No one can assume that they move "free floating" from a constructionist position and that they do not carry old baggage and unexamined assumptions in their minds, and they are likely to work better if they have a channel for these to emerge for scrutiny (Gorell Barnes, Down, & McCann, 2000). It is likely that genuine communication will be blocked, not only by the inherent power inequalities involved in any relationship between client and professional, but also by the assumptions each may have of how a person of the other's gender, ethnicity, and culture should behave and how they, as a man or woman, girl or boy, should respond. Misunderstandings will also arise from the professional's lack of awareness about issues from the client's world that are likely to be crucial to the client's own understanding of her/himself. One of my earliest experiences of being perceived as a racist professional was a clash with an African-Caribbean mother in 1967. She had to go into hospital for an operation and had applied to have her children taken into short-term care. Her husband hovered in the background while she spoke. I asked about his availability, and she brushed this aside. My senior (white male) believed that her husband (who was the children's father) should be encouraged to take time off work and care for the twins (good for male bonding, good for new sensitive fathering development, good for attachment). The mother was furious, saying that her husband "could not take time off work" and accusing me of racism because I did not want to provide the care of the state for her black babies. We were both very upset. At a later point in our meetings, a common bond of "women worrying about what's best for children" overtook the earlier discourse of black/white misunderstanding. We cried and hugged each other (away from the presence of the men involved), and we then were able to look further into the "misunderstanding" and the different values and priorities lying behind it. (For further deconstruction of "race" in intercultural therapeutic practice see Gorell Barnes, 1994, 1998; Hardy & Laszloffy, 1994; Thomas, 1995b.)

Do's and don'ts

I have written as asked about the "personal", and my notes about what is unwritten are now as long as the chapter itself. I say this because there is no answer to the title of this chapter: there is only the personal journey for each of us. However, from my own journey I would like to offer the following thoughts:

- Make sure you have at least one friend of a different "ethnicity" from your own to

    —check out stereotypical attitudes or ideas that are making you uneasy or/and

    —make you aware of how you are yourself taking on a position or attitude that needs further thought.

- Consider how challenging your family in relation to racist or stereotypical attitudes would free you from positions you don't like. Find a friend to help you work out how to go about it.
- Don't defer to older people just because they are "the older generation" if they are promoting racist attitudes. Let them know that these are outdated ideas that have no current place. Do this as often as is necessary in all contexts, politely but firmly and with closure.

- Don't defer to orthodoxy or zealotry of any kind when belief moves into a fundamentalist position that implicitly allows the destruction of those who are "not with us".
- Don't allow acts of speech that trivialize or minimize the individuality of human beings by grouping them in dismissive ways.
- *Do* keep your awareness of racism alive and documented, so that by confronting them with evidence you can continue to undermine those who deny that racism exists.
- *Do* assume that you will have to do these and other things, oriented towards seeing human beings and their rights clearly, for the rest of your life.

CHAPTER 10

Risky business: the rewards and demands of cross-cultural working with colleagues

Liz Burns & Charmaine Kemps

This chapter is born out of our experience as colleagues attempting to work together across cultures on the subject of culture and ethnicity. We hope that our experience informs the working relationship between professionals and clients, but our main intention in this chapter is to address issues raised in peer-professional working partnerships. We have chosen to speak with our personal voices, sometimes separately and sometimes together, in the hope that this will convey what we think is the value of our experience. The liberty has also been taken of addressing the reader directly from time to time. It is our belief that directness is often an important part of crossing the barriers in transcultural working. Our hindsight learning is boxed up here in the form of recommendations for practice.

In the autumn of 1999 we heard of the conference "Exploring the Unsaid" and decided to present a workshop, expecting it to be along the lines of an intellectual and professional debate on "An invitation to explore institutionalized categories of ethnic and cultural identity with a view to releasing more creative and respectful possibilities". We wanted to offer something on the cutting edge of practice but found ourselves instead on the dangerously sharp knife-edge of cross-cultural living. Our expectation was that we would have something interesting to say because we were taking a critical look at descriptive categories from two systemically informed, but ethnically distinct, viewpoints. We now think that the journey we undertook in our quest to be true to ourselves while planning the workshop reflects the title of the conference vividly enough to form the main focus of this chapter.

During the planning process, we were often faced with the dilemma of speaking our minds at the risk of upsetting or offending the other. The consequences of these communications between us, we found, were painfully unpredictable, leaving us with more dilemmas and risks in attempting to resolve our differences. It felt increasingly as though we were entering a fearful and challenging domain, which was, nevertheless, deeply significant for each of us, both as individuals and as members of cultural groups.

At the workshop itself, we greatly appreciated the many interesting contributions of the participants, but it was clear that, for us, the focus of our workshop had shifted significantly towards more personal reflections on "speaking the unsaid". We therefore felt it essential to allude to the difficulties we had encountered in preparation. We were not, at that stage, in a position to articulate our experience, and so the participants were left curious and wanting explanation. In this chapter we hope to describe and offer some understanding of the dilemmas and risks that we encountered in our attempt to offer a workshop on cross-cultural working.

Considerations for practice

- Before you embark on a piece of cross-cultural work requiring collaboration, whether with colleagues or with clients, it is important to decide the level of your expected commitment to each other and to the task, especially if, and when, the going gets difficult.

- The level of your commitment will need to be considered in the light of the emotional and interpersonal risks of being honest with each other about your thoughts if, and when, you fear upsetting and undermining the other. Disagreements and discomfort, if not dealt with, will become a barrier between you.

- Agreement about how you will communicate with each other if there are feelings of hurt or misunderstanding will help when there are difficulties.

- Ask yourselves if there should be a point beyond which you will not go.

Background

We are two women of broadly similar age and social status who work as family therapists in child and family psychiatric services in adjacent areas of Buckinghamshire. Charmaine is of Asian origin and from a first-generation immigrant family. Her father's ancestors were Dutch colonizers of Ceylon. Liz is, to the best of her knowledge, of European stock, from an English family. Our original intention was to present our own differences and to explore their creative potential. The most relevant difference was ethnic. Awareness of the complexity implied by descriptions such as "Asian", "European", "black", "white", and "other" had already made us eager to explore the subject in more detail in a workshop.

Initial discussions involved sharing our personal perspectives on the assumption that the other would not only understand, but also agree. This assumption was based on our belief that this would be essentially an intellectual exercise, and that our common training in family therapy and current professional positions would underpin the enterprise, providing a safe framework for exploration.

Too much difference can become divisive

As we attempted to negotiate the main themes and "spirit" of the workshop from our different positions, we became aware that the ideas that we had each held about our commonality and shared purpose were constantly eroded and challenged due to the misleading assumptions we held about each other and our own beliefs. A small, but highly significant, example of this awareness came when Liz made some initial notes that included the notion that "we are moving rapidly towards a multicultural society". When she read this, Charmaine wondered which "society" Liz was living in—she was already right in the middle of multicultural living! This difference of emphasis had previously been hidden, and each position had been taken for granted.

> *Considerations for practice*
>
> - Be aware (and beware!) of assumptions and presumptions in the context of shared projects, especially when working cross-culturally.
>
> - Knowing each other in your personal and professional roles will not guarantee similar perspectives on projects not previously attempted together. We think that this applies whether or not there is inequality of power between participants—that is, whether in work with clients or with colleagues.

These episodes of recognition were acutely uncomfortable and affected all areas of our relationship. For example, Charmaine felt committed to maintaining a position based on a deeply personal, genuine expression of her immigrant experience and of the process of acculturation in which she had experienced being institutionally categorized and marginalized. Liz, on the other hand, was currently preoccupied with understanding the experience of ethnic, cultural, and other differences through the cultural expressions of individuals and groups in writing and film. This approach had become important to her because she was, and is, intensely involved in an academic study of personal and professional development through the reading of literature. On reflection, we have come to characterize this bifurcation as a distinction between "insider" versus "outsider", or between differential levels of engagement, especially in terms of emotional investment. These differing perspectives effectively created conflict, not only between our points of view, but also between ourselves as people and as workshop presenters. As we attempted to negotiate some middle ground (mostly using email), we found ourselves in symmetrical positions and increasingly entrenched in opposition to each other over various planning details and content of the workshop. The more threatened we felt, the more we needed to defend our position, at times for fear of being overwhelmed and consumed by the other. In other circumstances, we might well have agreed to differ.

> *Considerations for practice*
>
> - Be aware that your training has probably not addressed emotional aspects of cross-cultural working.
> - Be prepared for unpredictable differences that take you by surprise. They are likely to be deeply embedded in past professional, personal, family, social, political, and cultural experiences and to be emotionally loaded.

Our conflict highlights and generates complexity

This conflict of positions—insider/outsider, intellectual/emotional—drew in meanings from other contexts that created complexity in our communication, and we think that this is most usefully presented in our separate voices. Attempting to write this chapter has involved us in exploring various styles and themes. We include those that we think will resonate with the experience of others in working cross-culturally. It seems important, also, to convey some of the emotional tone of our experience, although this continues to be a risk for us as two women who need to keep our relationship intact, and not jeopardize it for the sake of reviving memories for the purpose of writing this chapter! We hope that our conversation, though specific and personal to us, will give some indications of possible ways forward for others who find cross-cultural working not only stimulating and rewarding, but also, sometimes, a fearful activity.

> *Considerations for practice*
>
> - There are many socially sanctioned ways to avoid discomfort and disagreement—walking away, changing the subject, pretending you agree when you really disagree, and so on.

Cross-cultural working demands that you decide whether to take these options or risk commitment.

- Once you have made a commitment to each other and the task, be prepared to take risks in confronting the discomfort and disagreement together if you want to explore greater depths.
- If you expect your clients/colleagues to confront their differences, then your willingness to take these risks lends authority to your role and expectations as a leader/facilitator.
- Opportunities to take these risks are likely to occur at unpredictable moments.

CHARMAINE: A major source of discomfort for me in our struggle to define our differences was my perception that you had adopted an objective, intellectual position towards the subject of ethnicity and identity which you seemed to have mostly derived from literature and your academic studies. An example of this was your apparent preoccupation with the poetry and prose of black African-American and British writers. I thought you showed an unwarranted reliance upon these in approaching the workshop. This seemed incongruous with what I thought I knew about you as a person, and I began to experience a sense of alienation, as if my lived experience was not as important as those in literature. In contrast, my own beliefs about ethnicity were embedded in deeply personal experiences in which I, as an Asian woman, had no choice but to make sense of my own journey through prejudice and discrimination. I was not reading about my experience, I was living it. Yours seemed to be formed through other people's experiences. My need was to know how the writings of people "out there" related to the forming of your own personal ethnic identity, as a white, English, middle-class woman. I know that it was not your intention, but these feelings and thoughts triggered various other meanings from other contexts, which added complexity to our communication.

By this stage, I began to question whether my "authentic" minority ethnic status was only useful for the purpose of promoting an academic position. You were not to know this, but I had often protested, in previous learning contexts, when I thought that ethnicity was taught through "tokenism", the main ingredients of which seemed to be the presence of someone from an ethnic-minority group while the dominant teaching partner was white, English. At this point, we seemed locked in a repeating pattern of misunderstanding. I believe that this was an instance of the "strange loop" described by Cronen, Johnson, and Lannamann (1982) under the rubric of "co-ordinated management of meaning". There is no doubt in my mind that our language and meanings had become influenced by other levels of contexts—mine, from world history and my own background, which triggered thoughts of colonizers and the colonized; of the power to dominate, and the dominated; to use and be used. My personal experiences of institutional categorizations (our workshop theme), together with the conference title, challenged me to take the risk of exploring the unsaid, in our relationship across cultures, and telling you about my fears of being a token and of being exploited. This invoked fear of offending you, of being judged, and of losing our professional relationship. Faced with these dilemmas, and scared of the unpredictable and unknown, I held my first (as it turned out later) breath and took the plunge of letting you into my mind, with only a thread of hope that you would be able to hear this without it sounding like an awful personal criticism, offending your academic position and personhood.

Liz: In responding to your concerns, I first need to acknowledge that I find entirely reasonable your reservations about combining personal perspectives with those that are more distanced, perhaps more intellectualized and "academic". There is a real danger of devaluing the personal, the "insider" experience, by simply placing it alongside something that is derived from an "outsider" perspective. I agree that this may link with tokenism. I also acknowledge that your "gut feeling" about this was an invaluable source of guidance for us both during our struggle towards the workshop. I was very unhappy to hear that you suspected that I was using the workshop and your ethnic identity as a means of promoting myself, or an "academic" viewpoint, with the result of reproducing a colonial, even imperial, situation all over again. I had to ask myself, however, if there was not some grain of truth in what you alleged. Did my behaviour really betray intentions so different from what I proclaimed? Might a tendency to racial discrimination persist in my genes? Could I be so lacking in awareness and sensitivity? Though clear in my own mind that genes do not carry such tendencies, that ethnic differences and social behaviour are not biologically determined, I was nevertheless aghast at your perception of me and my intentions. I felt undermined and emotionally battered. This was exactly the reverse of what I had intended by undertaking the workshop. I could not help noticing, however, that our situation resembled other potentially problematic experiences of cross-cultural working, in which I, and others, had previously found solutions by decreasing the intensity of the situation, by walking away, or by retreating further into a theoretical mode. We were already in conflict because you thought my approach too theoretical, so this was no solution. An approaching deadline increased the intensity and anxiety of our communication.

Fortunately, through intense and frank—if upsetting—discussions, we were able to rediscover and clarify our shared commitment to seeing the workshop through. By maintaining open communication, both in person and by email, we were able to develop a greater understanding, without either of us having to abandon our dignity and sense of identity. An important part of this was, as you say, learning to acknowledge and share our own vulnerabilities. The more we were able to be honest with each other and to show that we were able to hear alternative perspectives and respond to them, the more we could establish an atmosphere of mutual trust.

As a white (how I mistrust the spurious inclusivity and the simultaneous overload, yet poverty, of meanings in that term!) person living in Britain, I have not so far experienced discrimination on grounds of ethnicity. I have no personal experience of migration and the devastating loss that this entails. I can only be an outsider to that reality. My response has been to seek understanding by trying to attend to the voices of others who are "insiders". It is important to me not only to hear voices that remain unheard because they are weak, but also to listen to those that express strength. So, I am keen to hear "grass-roots" expressions of shared personal realities, such as those produced by the

Sheffield-based MAMA East African Women's Group (MAMA, 1995), as well as to listen to powerful voices who interpret the marginalization and powerlessness of people for all the world to hear (Morrison, 1987; Walker, 1982). Cultural critics are also important (hooks, 1992; Morrison, 1992; Young, 1996), as are writers who offer compassionate, critical, or humorous insider views on a variety of everyday concerns (Kay, 1991; Nichols, 1984; Syal, 1997; Zephaniah, 1996). For me, this is not a substitute for personal experience but more a means of helping me understand my place in the world alongside others.

We live in a plural, post-colonial world where differences may be valued for themselves and accepted hierarchies can, and should, be questioned and overturned. It is fascinating to see, with hindsight, how each of us felt at a disadvantage relative to the other. I felt that, in the context of the conference, my position was the more vulnerable and that, as a white person, I really had to work hard to come up with something acceptable to the people there. Partly, my feeling of vulnerability derived from a lack of first-hand experience of racial discrimination, enforced migration, and dispossession, leading in my own mind to a sense of inauthenticity in respect of the experience that I do have of my own ethnicity and culture. I was not sure that I could come up with a valid contribution, even when presenting with you, Charmaine. On my own, I was sure that I could not.

> *Considerations for practice*
>
> - It is possible to work through complexities productively. We think it is worth persevering.
>
> - Past experiences always remain as a residue in the present and may be triggered when we least expect them, in a word or a sentence in a situation of stress or tension. This can lead to very complicated, perhaps confusing communication exactly at the moment when clarity is most important.
>
> - Be aware that expectations generated in wider political and social systems and/or an element of "public performance" (like running a workshop) can increase anxiety and confusion.

- There are no "right" answers to the questions posed in cross-cultural working.

- You, and those with whom you are collaborating, must feel free to question what has been taken for granted.

- You need to feel able to reveal and share vulnerabilities. Only in this way can you go on to evolve new positions that are more responsive to the demands of cross-cultural working.

CHARMAINE: Your reflections are interesting and thought provoking. Looking back, and even as we have collaborated for the purpose of this chapter, I have a sense that risking exposure, though painful, has enriched our understanding of the emotional commitment required in working effectively across cultural barriers. We have learned, during the process, to feel confident in the validity of our respective positions and to appreciate the fit between our different personal experiences. Crucially, we have gained courage in acknowledging the emotional impact of cross-cultural working. How would it have been different if we had both been of similar or different minority ethnic populations? We represent a partnership between dominant and minority cultures, but we have hypothesized that this is complex and includes individual personalities, as well as social and personal histories.

I have appreciated your sensitivity, openness, and honesty, which made it more possible to continue with my "gut feelings" than abandon them, but this did not make it easier to accommodate to your responses. For example, I was surprised by and unready to hear you reveal the complex processes that you and others have put yourselves through as "outsiders" to the minority experience in an effort to find your place in the world alongside others. I had never before, in a working relationship, as opposed to hearing someone speak from a teaching platform, heard a white English person acknowledge vulnerability on the subject of ethnicity. (I make no apology for continuing to use the "spurious" white construct: it is no different from terms such as the all-encompassing "black" or "other" labels that we had hoped to explore.)

Considerations for practice

- Descriptive categories based on skin colour cannot be taken as indicators of personal identity in the context of multicultural or multiracial living. People with "white" skin who have not previously felt called upon to think of themselves as owning an ethnic identity can no longer take the meaning of "white" for granted.
- All personal identities contain an ethnic dimension.
- Ethnicity is a universal experience, whatever the colour of one's skin
- "Insider/outsider" experiences and all they that entail do not, nevertheless, occur exclusively in relation to ethnicity, and cultural distinctions between people are not always signalled by skin colour, language, dress.

CHARMAINE: I think I must have appeared very insensitive and slow to respond to your acknowledgement of vulnerability and disadvantage when speaking on the subject of ethnicity. Preoccupation with my own preconceptions and dilemmas had to be peeled away before I could even vaguely register and hear your concerns about presenting this workshop, from an "outsider perspective". I had not previously needed to explore the vacuum of meaning in "whiteness" within an emotional relationship or space. Whenever I had addressed the folly of using colour as descriptions of ethnic identity, it had been from a distant-speaker's platform, not while living side by side with a "white" English person. With the benefit of hindsight, I realize that I had been acting on my assumptions and beliefs about you, in your professional, intellectual, and academic capacity, from which I had created an image of you as a very confident, competent, and capable woman. What I began to hear was that these virtues, by themselves, were unable to equip you to speak confidently on the subject of ethnicity with or without me. I have found this hard to grasp.

I am very curious to know how being confronted by and having to struggle with my "personal, insider minority" views influenced your thinking. To what extent, if any, did your thoughts shift from being one who is engaged in cultural discourses about ethnicity and culture to one who speaks as much from your insider English/European perspective? I ask this because it seemed to me that our positions had shifted, and we were united in risking exposure of our emotions and intellect. Beliefs, assumptions, theories, and academic and intellectualizing voices were subjected to personal as well as intellectual scrutiny. It was as if we had entered a theatre stage, by agreement to doing the workshop, but once the lights went on we were compelled by the director to discard our neatly preconceived original scripts and become co-authors and players in an unrehearsed spontaneous dialogue about our ethnic identities, and each other's sensitivities. This unpredictable exposure was very threatening, but I think it became a creative tension between us.

LIZ: I think that the metaphor of a public performance helps me to see more clearly the interrelationship of interior and exterior processes—the private and the public. This seems to me to relate closely to the insider/outsider debate, which I think we both initially conceived as dichotomous—that is, we must be either insiders or outsiders, that the terms are mutually exclusive and must be in opposition. The feeling of being an outsider tends to undermine confidence, to make one's own experience feel inauthentic, of less value than that of the insider. The prospect of public performance (the workshop) magnified this feeling for me, to the detriment of understanding that an outsider's experience is inevitably different but not necessarily inferior or "unreal". Going through the public performance together has helped me to re-value my own personal experience partly through making clearer distinctions between different ways of knowing about ethnic and cultural differences, and by reminding me of the dangers of talking indiscriminately across categories (Bateson, 1972), or discourses as we might now want to name them—as though, for example, an insider perspective were the same as an outsider perspective, a cultural perspective were the same as a biological one, the map the same as the territory (Bateson, 1972). We also know that the personal is always to some extent political, but what

I found myself beginning to see is that we lump different ways of "knowing" together at our peril, especially when we try to engage with complex and sensitive topics in conversation with others who have different vantage points. I need to recognize the authenticity and relevance of my "insider" identity (even if some of the descriptions are irksome—as you say "white" is no emptier nor misleadingly full than "black" or "other") in order to talk meaningfully with you about yours.

> *Considerations for practice*
>
> - "Insider" or "outsider" positions are defined by social context, and, while both perspectives are equally valid, and may often overlap, it is essential to own the position you adopt as a basic starting position.
> - Wherever possible, try to distinguish between professional/ personal positions, characteristics, and behaviour and the intrinsic identity of the person.
> - It is important to honour your own experience as a basis on which to take a position.
> - You may legitimately want to engage with cross-cultural working to a greater or lesser extent. Not being clear about the position you are taking can be confusing and offensive and may endanger the partnership, while respect for difference in genuine, personal experience can help move the process along.

Liz: In one of our many recent conversations, I recollected with you the experience of some antiracist training in the early 1980s. I told you how uncomfortable these groups could be, seeming to carry the overarching message that people of different skin colour and cultural heritages could not sit down together without confrontation, guilt, and a sense of dangerousness. However justified this message may have been in challenging assumptions, raising consciousness, and highlighting oppressive practices, the fact that it promoted anxiety and often silenced genuine debate was, I believe, ultimately unhelpful. I think that we are reaping some of what we have sown in the family therapy world when we see that many practitioners, seeking to work cross-culturally, are content to consider only power inequalities between cultural groups and to think that if we give clients—the powerless—from ethnic minorities some of our power (a logical impossibility, we know) then we will be successful and ethical in our working. This entirely misses the complexity and richness potential in cross-cultural working by continuing to recognize only power inequalities as relevant to difference between people. I think I have been helped to move from this position very much as a consequence of our efforts.

Conclusion

We were surprised to find, through working together on the workshop and subsequently this chapter, the differences between talking face to face, talking through emails, and talking and writing together. Communicating via emails without the social signals that are useful in reading the other person's reactions sometimes moved us further apart, whereas talking at the same time as writing together helped us find a form for more creative and coherent collaboration. Our experience suggests that emailing from separate positions was useful if we wanted to encourage free expression, whereas talking and writing together focused our minds and brought our thinking together. The exercise of producing this chapter was enriched by our conscious preference for "both/and" as opposed to "either/or" perspectives, but this preference for inclusiveness needed to be balanced by clarity and honesty about the specific nature of the positions taken. We understood our experience more fully through writing and thinking about it together, so it may be useful to experiment with jointly constructing a written "manifesto", or other permanent record of intention, as an adjunct to a piece of cross-cultural working.

Our aim has been to demonstrate the emotional and interpersonal rewards and demands of working with colleagues across cultural and personal boundaries, in the belief that our clients are best served when we are authentic, genuine to ourselves and others, and work consciously from an ethical position. On reflection, we recognize that efforts to protect our own positions presented us with ethical dilemmas and tested our assumptions that our lives were safely embedded in sound ethical principles, such as the individual's right to autonomy, fairness, non-maleficence—that is, above all, doing no harm (Zygmond & Boorhem, 1989). Striking the right balance between protecting and elevating the "I/my" as against the "you/your" status required us to accept that ethical positions exist in the context of relationships. Ethical texts are not cosy, or easy to live out in practice, when one's own space or ideas are threatened. What we wonder is, does our experience reflect the conflict that our clients experience if they feel under threat or facing oppression? If it does, then we think it all the more important to hold on to ethical principles to guide us through the personal/professional difficulties in working sensitively across ethnic and cultural differences.

REFERENCES

Ahmed, S., et al. (Eds.) (1986). *Social Work with Black Children and Their Families*. London: Batsford/BAAF.

Albee, G. W. (1982). Preventing psychopathology and human potential. *American Psychologist*, 37: 1043–1050.

Allen, D. (1997). Social construction of self: some Asian, Marxist, and feminist critiques of dominant Western views of self. In D. Allen (Ed.), *Culture and Self: Philosophical and Religious Perspectives, East and West*. Colorado: Westview Press.

Anderson, H., & Goolishian, H. (1992). The client is the expert: a not-knowing approach to therapy. In: S. McNamee & K. Gergen (Eds.), *Therapy as Social Construction*. London: Sage.

Arnold, E. (1974). "Mourning and Attachment: African Caribbean Women and Their Children." Unpublished M.Phil Dissertation [now Ph.D. in preparation, UCL], Woodberry Down Child Guidance Clinic.

Azuma, H. (1984). Psychology in a non-Western country. *International Journal of Psychology*, 19: 145–155.

Baker, J. (1999). "Lest We Forget—The Children They Left Behind: The Life Experiences of Adults Born to Black GIs and British Women during the Second World War." Unpublished MSW Thesis, School of Social Work, Faculty of Arts, University of Melbourne.

Banks, N. (1999). *White Counsellors, Black Clients.* Aldershot: Ashgate.

Barn, R. (1993). *Black Children in the Public Care System.* London: Batsford.

Barn, R. (1998). Race and racism: can minority ethnic groups benefit from social work. In: J. Edwards & J. P. Revauger (Eds.), *Discourse on Inequality in France and Britain.* Aldershot: Ashgate.

Barn, R. (1999). White mothers, mixed-parentage children and child welfare. *British Journal of Social Work, 29* (2).

Barn, R. (2000). Race, ethnicity and transracial adoption. In: I. Katz & A. Treacher (Eds.), *The Dynamics of Adoption.* London: Jessica Kingsley.

Barn, R., & Sinclair, R. (1999). Black families and children: planning to meet their needs. *Journal of Research, Policy and Planning, 17* (2): 5–1.

Barn, R., Sinclair, R., & Ferdinand, D. (1997). *Acting on Principle: An Examination of Race and Ethnicity in Social Services Provision for Children and Families.* London: British Agencies for Adoption and Fostering.

Bateson, G. (1972). *Steps to an Ecology of Mind.* New York: Ballantine Books; St. Albans: Paladin, 1973.

Bebbington, A. C., & Miles, J. B. (1989). The background of children who enter local authority care. *British Journal of Social Work, 19* (5): 349–368.

Boyd-Franklin, N. (1989). *Black Families in Therapy: A Multi-Systems Approach.* New York: Guilford.

Brock, G. W. (1997). Reducing vulnerability to ethics code violations: an at-risk test for marriage and family therapists. *Journal of Marital and Family Therapy, 23* (No. 1, Jan.): 87–89.

Burck, C., & Speed, B. (Eds.) (1995). *Gender, Power and Relationships.* London: Routledge.

Burke, A. (1997). "The Dysfunctional Family in the Black Community: Causes and Consequences." Paper presented at annual conference, *Black Mental Health,* of Association of Black Psychologists (London, 12 July).

Burman, E., Gowrisunkur, J., & Sangha, K. (1998). Conceptualising cultural and gendered identities in psychological therapies. *European Journal of Psychotherapy, Counselling and Health, 2:* 231–256.

Butt, J., & Box, L. (1998). *Family Centred: A Study of the Use of Family Centres by Black Families*. London: REU.
Byng-Hall, J. (1995). *Re-writing Family Scripts: Improvisation and Systems Change*. London: Guilford.
Cacas, J. M. (1984). Policy, training, and research in counselling psychology: the racial/ethnic minority perspective. In: S. D. Brown & R. W. Lent (Eds.), *Handbook of Counselling Psychology* (pp. 785–831). New York: Wiley.
Caesar, G., Parchment, M., & Berridge, D. (1994). *Black Perspectives on Services for Children and in Need*. London: National Children's Bureau.
Carby, H. (1982). Schooling in Babylon. In: Centre for Contemporary Cultural Studies, *The Empire Strikes Back: Race and Racism in 70s Britain*. London: Hutchinson.
Carter, B., & McGoldrick, M. (Eds.) (1989). *The Changing Life Cycle: A Framework for Family Therapy*. New York: Allyn & Bacon.
Carter, R. T. (1997). Race and psychotherapy: the racially inclusive model. In: C. E. Thompson & R. T. Carter (Eds.), *Racial Identity Theory: Applications to Individual, Group, and Organizational Interventions* (pp. 97–112). Mahwah, NJ: Lawrence Erlbaum.
Cecchin, G., Lane, G., & Ray, W. A. (Eds.) (1994). *The Cybernetics of Prejudices in the Practice of Psychotherapy*. London: Karnac.
Cecchin, G., Lane, G., & Ray, W. A. (1992). *Irreverence: A Strategy for Therapists' Survival*. London: Karnac.
Chand, A. (2000). The over-representation of black children in the child protection system: possible causes, consequences and solutions. *Child and Family Social Work*, 5: 67–77.
Cheetham, J. (1981a). *Social Work Services for Ethnic Minorities in Britain and the USA*. London: Department of Health and Social Security.
Cheetham, J. (Ed.) (1981b). *Social and Community Work in a Multi-Racial Society*. London: Harper & Row.
Cheetham, J. (Ed.) (1982). *Social Work and Ethnicity*. London: Allen & Unwin.
Cooklin, A. (Ed.) (1999). *Changing Organisations: Clinicians as Agents of Change*. London: Karnac.
Cooklin, A. & Barnes, G. G. (1994). The shattered picture of the family: encountering new dimensions of human relations, of the family, and of therapy. In V. Sinason (Ed.), *Treating Survivors of Satanist Abuse* (pp. 120–130). New York: Routledge.

Corey, G., Schneider-Corey, M., & Callanan, P. (1992). *Issues and Ethics in the Helping Professions* (4th edition). Pacific Grove, CA: Brooks/Cole.

Cronen, V., Johnson, K., & Lannamann, J. (1982). Paradoxes, double binds and reflexive loops: an alternative theoretical perspective. *Family Process, 21*: 91–112.

Cross, W. E. Jr. (1995). Oppositional identity and African American youth: Issues and prospects. In: W. D. Hawley & A. W. Jackson (Eds.), *Toward a Common Destiny: Improving Race and Ethnic Relations in America* (pp. 185–204). San Francisco, CA: Jossey-Bass.

d'Ardenne, P., & Mahtani, A. (1999). *Transcultural Counselling in Action* (2nd edition). Thousand Oaks, CA: Sage.

Department of Health (1991). *The Children Act 1989. Guidance and Regulations*. London: HMSO.

Department of Health (2000). *The Children Act Report. Cm4579*. London: HMSO.

Dewey, J. (1929). The quest for certainty. In *John Dewey: The Later Works, 1925–1953, Vol. 4: 1929*, ed. J. A. Boydston. Carbondale, IL: University of Southern Illinois Press, 1984.

Divine, D. (1983). Defective, hypocritical and patronising research. *Caribbean Times*, 4 March.

Douglas, M., & Ney, S. (1998). *Missing Persons: A Critique of Personhood in the Social Sciences*. Berkeley, CA: University of California Press.

Du Bois, W. E. B. (Ed.) (1906). *The Health and Physique of the North American Negro*. Atlanta, GA: Atlanta University Press.

Dutt, R., & Phillips, M. (1996). *Race, Culture and the Prevention of Child Abuse, Childhood Matters, Vol. 2*. National Commission of Inquiry into the Prevention of Child Abuse. London: HMSO.

Dutt, R., & Phillips, M. (2000). Assessing black children in need and their families. In: *Assessing Children in Need and Their Families*. London: Department of Health.

Dyche, L., & Zayas, L. (1995). The value of curiosity and naivete for the cross-cultural therapist. *Family Process, 34*: 389–399.

Family Welfare Association (1958). *The West Indian Comes to England*. London: Routledge & Kegan Paul, 1960.

Fatimilehin, I., & Coleman, P. (1998). Appropriate services for African-Caribbean families: views from one community. *Clinical Psychology Forum, 118*: 6–11.

Fernando, S. (1988). *Race, Culture and Psychiatry*. London: Routledge.

Fernando, S. (Ed.) (1995a). *Mental Health in a Multi-ethnic Society.* London: Routledge.
Fernando, S. (1995b). Social realities and mental health. In: S. Fernando (Ed.), *Mental Health in a Multi-Ethnic Society: A Multidisciplinary Handbook* (pp. 11–49). London: Routledge.
Fitzherbert, K. (1967). *West Indian Children in London,* London: Bell & Sons.
Flaskas, C., & Perlesz, A. (Eds.) (1996). *The Therapeutic Relationship in Systemic Therapy.* London: Karnac.
Fordham, M. (1974). Defenses of the self. *Journal of Analytical Psychology, 9* (2): 192–199.
Fruggeri, L. (1992). Therapeutic process as the social construction of change. In: S. McNamee & K. J. Gergen (Eds.), *Therapy as Social Construction* (pp. 40–53). London: Sage.
Furnham, A., & Bocher, S. (1988). *Culture Shock.* London: Sage.
Geertz, C. (1974). From the native's point of view. *Bulletin of the American Academy of Arts and Sciences, 28* (1).
Gellner, E. (1998). *Language and Solitude: Wittgenstein, Malinowski and the Habsburg Dilemma.* Cambridge: Cambridge University Press.
Gibbons, J., et al. (1995). *Operating the Child Protection System.* London: HMSO.
Gill, O., & Jackson, B. (1983). *Adoption and Race.* London: Batsford/BAAF.
Gorell Barnes, G. (1975). Seen but not heard: work with West Indian clients and their families. *Social Work Today* (Issues 20–22).
Gorell Barnes, G. (Ed.) (1994). Ethnicity, culture, race and family therapy. *Context, 20.*
Gorell Barnes, G. (1995). Gender. In: K. Davie, G. Upton, & V. Varma (Eds.), *The Voice of the Child.* Basingstoke: Farmer Press.
Gorell Barnes, G. (1998). *Family Therapy in Changing Times.* Basingstoke: Macmillan.
Gorell Barnes, G., Down, G., & McCann, D. (2000). *Systemic Supervision: A Portable Model.* London: Jessica Kingsley.
Haley, J. (1996). *Learning and Teaching Therapy.* New York: Guilford Press.
Hall, C. C. I. (1997). Cultural malpractice: the growing obsolescence of psychology with the changing US population. *American Psychologist, 52*: 642–651.
Hall, E. T. (1983). *The Dance of Life.* New York: Doubleday.

Harding, S. (1987). *Feminism and Methodology: Social Science Issues*. Milton Keynes: Open University Press.

Hardy, K., & Laszloffy, T. (1994). Deconstructing race in family therapy. *Journal of Feminist Family Therapy*, 3 (4): 5–33.

Haste, H. (1987). Growing into rules. In J. Bruner & H. Haste (Eds.), *The Child's Construction of the World*. London: Methuen.

Hawkes, B. (1995). The meaning of home hairdressing and its cultural uses in the African Caribbean community. *Journal of Black Therapy*, 1 (1).

Helms, J. E., & Carter, R. T. (1991). Relationships of White and Black racial identity attitudes and demographic similarity to counselor preferences. *Journal of Counseling Psychology*, 38 (4): 446–457.

Henriques, J. (1984). Social psychology and the politics of racism. In J. Henriques, W. Hollway, C. Urwin, & V. Walkerdine (Eds.), *Changing the Subject: Psychology, Social Regulation and Subjectivity*. London & New York: Routledge.

Hildebrand, J. (1998). *Bridging the Gap: A Training Module in Personal and Professional Development*. London: Karnac.

Ho, D. Y. F. (1993). Relational orientation in Asian social psychology. In U. Kim & J. W. Berry (Eds.), *Indigenous Psychologies*. Newbury Park, CA: Sage.

Hoffman, L. (1993). *Exchanging Voices: A Collaborative Approach to Family Therapy*. London: Karnac.

Holdstock, T. L. (2000). *Re-examining Psychology: Critical Perspectives and African Insights*. London: Routledge.

Holland, S. (1990). Psychotherapy, oppression and social action: gender, race and class in black women's depression. In: R. Perelberg & A. Miller (Eds.), *Gender and Power in Families*. London: Routledge.

hooks, b. (1992). *Black Looks: Race and Representation*. London: Turnaround.

Howe, D., & Hinings, D. (1987). Adopted children referred to a child and family centre. *Adoption and Fostering*, 11 (3): 44–47.

Huang, L. N. (1994). An integrative approach to clinical assessment and intervention with Asian-American adolescents. *Journal of Clinical Child Psychology*, 23: 21–31.

Humphries, C., Atkar, S., & Baldwin, N. (1999). Discrimination in child protection work: rRecurring themes in work with Asian families. *Child and Family Social Work*, 4: 283–291.

Hylton, C. (1997). *Black Families' Survival Strategies: Way of Coping in UK Society*. York: Joseph Rowntree Foundation.

Ince, L. (1998). *Making It Alone: A Study of the Care Experiences of Young Black People*. London: BAAF.

Jackson, G. G. (1980). The emergence of a black perspective in counselling. In: R. L. Jones (Ed.), *Black Psychology*. New York: Harper & Row.

Johnson, M. (1986). Citizenship, social work and ethnic minorities. In: S. Etherington (Ed.), *Social Work and Citizenship*. Birmingham: British Association of Social Workers.

Jones, A., & Butt, J. (1995). *Taking the Initiative: The Report of a National Study Assessing Service Provision to Black Families and Children*. London: NSPCC.

Jones, E. (1994). *Family Systems Therapy: Developments in the Milan-Systemic Therapies*. London: John Wiley.

Jung, C. G. (1930). Your negroid and Indian behavior. *Forum* (April). [Reprinted as "The complications of American psychology", in *Collected Works of C. G. Jung, Vol. 10* (p. 502–514). Princeton, NJ: Princeton University Press.]

Kakar, S. (1978). *The Inner World: A Psychoanalytic Study of Childhood and Society in India*. Delhi: Oxford University Press.

Kareem, J., & Littlewood, R. (1992). *Intercultural Therapy: Themes, Interpretations and Practice*. Oxford: Blackwell.

Kay, J. (1991). *The Adoption Papers*. Newcastle upon Tyne: Bloodaxe Books.

Knappert, K. (1995). *African Mythology: An Encyclopedia of Myth and Legend*. London: Diamond Books.

Kohut, H. (1971). *The Analysis of the Self*. New York: International Universities Press.

Kornreich, R., et al. (1973). "Social Workers' Attitudes towards Immigrant Clients." Unpublished summary of research project, School of Applied Social Studies, University of Bradford.

Krause, I.-B. (1998). *Therapy across Culture*. London: Sage.

Krause, I.-B. (2001). *Culture and System in Family Therapy*. London: Karnac.

Landrine, H. (1992). Clinical implications of cultural differences: the referential versus the indexical self. *Clinical Psychology Review*, 12: 401–415.

Lau, A. (1984). Transcultural issues in family therapy. *Journal of Family Therapy, 6*: 91–112.

Lau, A. (1988). Family therapy and ethnic minorities. In E. Street & W. Dryden (Eds.), *Family Therapy in Britain* (pp. 270–290). London: Open University Press.

Lau, A. (Ed.) (2000). *South Asian Children and Adolescents in Britain*. London: Collin Whurr.

Lawrence, E. (1982). *Common Sense, Racism and the Sociology of Race Relations*. Birminham: Centre for Contemporary Cultural Studies, Stencilled Occasional Paper, No. 66..

Leary, K. (1995). "Interpreting in the dark": race and ethnicity in psychoanalytic psychotherapy. *Psychoanalytic Psychology, 12* (1): 127–140.

Lee, C. (1991). Ethical principles and standards: a racial-ethnic minority research perspective. Comment. *Counselling and Values, 35* (No. 3, April): 200–202.

Lerner, M., & West, C. (1995). *Jews and Blacks*. New York: Putnam.

Lesser, R. C. (1996). All that's solid melts into air: deconstructing some psychoanalytic facts. *Contemporary Psychoanalysis, 32*: 5–23.

Levine, R. V., & Bartlett, C. (1984). Pace of life, punctuality and coronary heart disease in six countries. *Journal of Cross-Cultural Psychology, 15*: 233–255.

Lieberman, S. (1979). Transgenerational analysis: the geneogram as a technique in family therapy. *Journal of Family Therapy, 1*: 51–64.

Littlewood, R., & Lipsedge, M. (1989). *Aliens and Alienists: Ethnic Minorities and Psychiatry* (2nd edition). London: Unwin Hyman.

Lloyd, B. (1987). Social representations of gender. In: J. Bruner & H. Haste (Eds.), *The Child's Construction of the World*. London: Methuen.

Lomov, F. F., Budilova, E. A., Koltsova, V. A., & Medvedev, A. M. (1993). Psychological thought within the system of Russian culture. In: U. Kim & J. W. Berry (Eds.), *Indigenous Psychologies: Research and Experience in Cultural Context* (pp. 104–117). London: Sage.

Maccoby, E. E. (1980). *Social Development, Psychological Growth and the Parent Child Relationship*. New York: Harcourt Brace Jovanovich.

MacDonald, S. (1992). *All Equal under the Act?* London: Race Equalities Unit.

MacKinnon, L. (1998). *Trust and Betrayal in the Treatment of Child Abuse*. New York: Guilford.

Macpherson, Sir W. (1999). *The Stephen Lawrence Inquiry*. London: HMSO.

Maitra, B. (1996). Child abuse: a universal "diagnostic" category? The implication of culture in definition and assessment. *International Journal of Social Psychiatry, 42*: 287–304.

MAMA (1995). *Shells on a Woven Cord*. Castleford: Yorkshire Art Circus. [Reprinted *Context, 47* (2000): 13.]

Markus, H. R., & Kitayama, S. (1991). Culture and self: implications for cognition, emotion, and motivation. *Psychological Review, 98*: 224–253.

Mason, B. (1993). Towards positions of safe uncertainty. *Human Systems, 4*: 189–200.

Mazower, M. (1993). *Inside Hitler's Greece*. Newhaven, CT, & London: Yale University Press.

Mbiti, J. (1969). *African Religions and Philosophies*. London: Heinemann; New York: Anchor Books, 1970.

McCulloch, J., Batta, I., & Smith, N. (1979). Colour as a variable in the children's section of a local authority social services department. *New Community, 7*: 78–84.

McGee, D. P., & Clark, C. X. (1974). Critical elements of black mental health. *Journal of Black Health Perspectives, USA* (August): 52–58.

McGoldrick, M. (Ed.) (1998). *Re-Visioning Family Therapy: Race, Culture and Gender in Clinical Practice*. London: Guilford Press.

Messent, P., & Murrell, M. (forthcoming). Research leading to action: a study of accessibility of a child and mental health service to ethnic communities. *Child and Adolescent Mental Health*.

Miller, A., & Thomas, L. K. (1994). Introducing ideas about racism and culture into family therapy training. *Context, 20* (Autumn).

Modood, T., et al. (1997). *Ethnic Minorities in Britain*. London: Policy Studies Institute.

Moghaddam, F. (1993). Traditional and modern psychologies in competing cultural systems: lessons from Iran 1978–1981. In U. Kim & J. W. Berry (Eds.), *Indigenous Psychologies: Research and Experience in Cultural Context* (pp. 104–117). London: Sage.

Moncayo, R. (1998). Cultural diversity and the cultural and epistemological structure of psychoanalysis: implications for psychotherapy with Latinos and other minorities. *Psychoanalytic Psychology*, 15 (2): 262–286.

Montagu, A. (1974). *Man's Most Dangerous Myth: The Fallacy of Race*. New York: Oxford University Press; Wallnut Creek, CA: Altamira Press, 1997 (6th edition).

Morris, H. S. (1968). Ethnic groups. In: D. L. Skills (Ed.), *International Encyclopedia of the Social Sciences*, Vol. 5 (p. 167). New York: Macmillan.

Morrison, T. (1987). *Beloved*. London: Chatto & Windus.

Morrison, T. (1992). *Playing in the Dark: Whiteness and the Literary Imagination*. London: Harvard University Press.

National Children's Home (1954). The problem of the coloured child: the experience of the National Children's Home. *Child Care Quarterly*, 8 (2).

Neihart, M. (1999). Systematic risk-taking. *Roeper-Review*, 21 (No. 4, May–June): 289–292.

Nichols, G. (1984). *The Fat Black Woman's Poems*. London: Virago.

O'Brian, C. (1990). Family therapy with black families. *Journal of Family Therapy*, 12: 3–16.

Ochs, E., & Taylor, C. (1992). Family narrative as political activity. *Discourse and Society*, 3: 301–340.

Owusu-Bempah, J. (1997). Race: a framework for social work? In M. Davies (Ed.), *Blackwell Companion to Social Work*. Oxford: Blackwell.

Owusu-Bempah, K. (1999). Confidentiality and social work practice in African cultures. In: B. R. Compton and B. Gallaway (Eds.), *Social Work Processes* (6th ed., pp. 166–185). Pacific Grove, CA: Brooks/Cole.

Owusu-Bempah, K., & Howitt, D. (2000). *Psychology: Beyond Western Perspectives*. Leicester: British Psychological Society.

Page, R. C., & Berkow, D. N. (1991). Concepts of the self: Western and Eastern perspectives. *Journal of Multicultural Counselling and Development*, 19: 83–93.

Paniagua, F. A. (1994). *Assessing and Treating Culturally Diverse Clients: A Practice Guide*. London: Sage.

Paré, D. (1995). Of families and other cultures: the shifting paradigm of family therapy. *Family Process*, 34: 1–19.

Paré, D. (1996). Culture and meaning: expanding the metaphorical repertoire of family therapy. *Family Process*, 35: 21–42.

REFERENCES

Parker, W. M., Moore, M. A., & Neimeyer, G. J. (1998). Altering white racial identity and interracial comfort through multicultural training. *Journal of Counselling and Development*, 76: 302–310.

Peavy, R. V. (1996). Counselling as a cultural healing. *British Journal of Guidance and Counselling*, 24: 141–150.

Pedersen, P. (1997). *Culture-Centred Counselling Interventions: Striving for Accuracy*. Thousand Oaks, CA: Sage.

Penketh, L. (2000). *Tackling Institutional Racism*. London: The Policy Press.

Perelberg, R. J., & Miller, A. (Eds.) (1990). *Gender and Power in Families*. London: Routledge.

Qureshi, T., Berridge, D., & Wenman, H. (2000). *Where To Turn? Family Support for South Asian Communities—A Case Study*. London: National Children's Bureau/JRF.

Rashid, H., & Rashid, S. (2000). Similarities and differences: working respectfully with the Bangladeshi community. In: A. Lau (Ed.), *South Asian Children and Adolescents in Britain*, London: Whurr.

Richards, A., & Ince, L. (2000). *Overcoming the Obstacles, Looked After Children: Quality Services for Black and Minority Ethnic Children and Their Families*. London: Family Rights Group.

Richards, G. (2000). "Ethnic Matching in Counselling." Paper presented at conference held by British Psychological Society, Division of Counselling Psychology (Liverpool, 19–21 May).

Richeport-Haley, M. (1998). Ethnicity in family therapy: a comparison of brief stragic therapy and culture-focused therapy. *American Journal of Family Therapy*, 26: 77–90.

Robinson, L. (2000). Racial identity attitudes and self-esteem measures among African-Caribbean children in residential care. *British Journal of Social Work*, 30: 3–24.

Roland, A. (1997). How universal is psychoanalysis? The self in India, Japan, and the United States. In: D. Allen (Ed.), *Culture and Self: Philosophical and Religious Perspectives, East and West* (pp. 27–39). Boulder, CO: Westview Press.

Rossiter, A., Walsh-Bowers, R., & Prilleltensky, I. (1996). Learning from broken rules: individualism, bureaucracy, and ethics. *Ethics and Behavior*, 6 (4): 307–320.

Rowe, J., Hundleby, M., & Garnett, L. (1989). *Child Care Now*. London: BAAF, Research Series 6.

Rowe, J., & Lambert, L. (1973). *Children Who Wait*. London: Association of British Adoption Agencies.

Rushton, A., & Minnis, H. (2000). Research review: transracial placements—a commentary on a new adult outcome study. *Adoption and Fostering*, 24 (No. 1, Spring): 53–59.

Safaris, M., & Eve, M. (Eds.) (1990). *Background to Contemporary Greece*. London: Merlin Press.

Said, E. (1999). *Out of Place: A Memoir*. New York: Knopf.

Sassoon, S. (1919). *Poems Newly Selected*. London: Faber & Faber, 1940.

Sawyerr, A. (1999). Identity project on "myself" with pre-schoolers at a day nursery. In: R. Barn (Ed.), *Working with Black Children and Adolescents in Need*. London: BAAF.

Scarman, Lord (1982). *The Brixton Disorders, 10–12 April 1981*. Cmnd 8427. London: HMSO.

Shiang, J., Kjellander, C., Huang, K., & Bogumill, S. (1998). Developing cultural competency in clinical practice. *Clinical Psychology: Science and Practice*, 5 (2): 182–210.

Silavwe, G. W. (1995). The need for a new social work perspective in an African setting: the case of social casework in Zambia. *British Journal of Social Work*, 25: 71–84.

Simon, R. J., & Alstein, H. (1981) *Transracial Adoption: A Follow-Up*. Lexington, MA: D. C. Heath.

Small, J. (1984). The crisis in adoption, *International Journal of Psychiatry*, 30 (Spring): 129–142.

Smith, P. B., & Bond, M. H. (1993). *Social Psychology across Cultures*. Hemel Hempstead: Harvester Wheatsheaf.

Steadman, C. (1985). Listen, How the Caged Bird Sings: Amarjit's Song. In: C. Steadman, C. Urwin, & V. Walkerdine (Eds.), *Language, Gender and Childhood*. London: Routledge & Kegan Paul.

Sue, D. W., & Sue, D. (1999). *Counselling the Culturally Different: Theory and Practice* (3rd edition). NewYork: Wiley.

Sue, S. (1987). The role of culture and cultural techniques in psychotherapy: a critique and reformulation. *American Psychologist*, 42: 37–45.

Syal, M. (1997). *Anita and Me*. London: Flamingo.

Thoburn, J., Norford, L., & Rashid, S. (2000). *Permanent Family Placement for Children of Minority Ethnic Origin*. London: Jessica Kingsley.

Thomas, L. (1992). Racism and psychotherapy: working with racism in the consulting room: an analytical view. In: J. Kareem & R. Littlewood (Eds.), *Intercultural Therapy: Themes, Interpretations and Practice*. Oxford: Blackwell.

Thomas, L. (1995a). "Diversity in Child and Family Experience: Challenging Eurocentric Schemas." Unpublished paper presented at joint conference, *Working with Families in a Multi-Ethnic Society: Confronting Racism and Taking Account of Culture*, held by Institute of Family Therapy and Transcultural Psychiatry Society U.K., (30–31 January).

Thomas, L. (1995b). Psychotherapy in the context of race and culture: an intercultural therapeutic approach. In: S. Fernando (Ed.), *Mental Health in a Multi-Ethnic Society*. London: Routledge.

Thomas, L. (1996). Multi-cultural aspects of attachment. *British Association of Counseling, RACE Newsletter, 10* (May): 16–20.

Thomas, L. (2000). What cost assimilation and integration? Working with transcultural issues. In: C.-A. Hooper & U. McCluskey (Eds.), *Psychodynamic Perspectives on Abuse: The Cost of fear*. London: Jessica Kingsley.

Triandis, H. C. (1986). Collectivisn vs. individualism: a reconceptualization of a basic concept in cross-cultural psychology. In C. Bagley & K. Verma (Eds.), *Personality Cognition and Values: Cross-Cultural Perspectives of Childhood and Adolescence*. London: Macmillan.

Triandis, H. C. (1995). *Individualism and Collectivism*. Boulder, CO: Westview Press.

Wakefield, J. C. (1996). Does social work need the eco-systems perspective? Part 1: Is the perspective clinically useful? *Social Service Review, 70*: 1–32.

Walker, A. (1982). *The Colour Purple*. New York: Washington Square Press.

Watts-Jones, D. (1997). Towards an African-American genogram. *Family Process, 36*: 375–383.

Weidman, H. (1978). Falling-out. *Social Science and Medicine, 13*: 95–112.

White, M., & Epston, D. (1990). *Narrative Means to Therapeutic Ends*. New York: Norton.

Whyte, S. R. (1997). *Questioning Misfortune: The Pragmatics of Uncertainty in Uganda*. Cambridge: Cambridge University Press.

Wijsen, F. (1999). Beyond the fatal impact theory: globalization and its cultural underpinnings. In: M. Amaladoss (Ed.), *Globalization and Its Victims: As Seen by the Victims* (pp. 122–131). Delhi: Cambridge Press.

Wittgenstein, L. (1921). *Tractatus Logico-Philosophicus*, tr. D. F. Pears & B. F. McGuinness. London: Routledge, 1974.

Young, L. (1996). *Fear of the Dark: "Race", Gender and Sexuality in the Cinema*. London: Routledge.

Zephaniah, B. (1996). *Propa Propaganda*. Newcastle upon Tyne: Bloodaxe Books.

Zygmond, M. J., & Boorhem, H. (1989). Ethical decision making in family therapy. *Family Process, 28*: 269–280.

INDEX

abuse:
   emotional, 40
   physical, 8, 120
   of power, 108
      see also power
   sexual, 8, 9, 27, 57, 101–103
   verbal, 117, 119
acculturation, 142, 151
adolescents:
   inpatient psychiatric unit for, 85–94
   see also children
African Families Project, 69–81
aggression, 86, 88
Ahmed, S., 4
Albee, G. W., 24
Allen, D., 32
Alstein, H., 13
Anane-Agyei, A., 69–81
Anderson, H., 44
antiracist practices, 12, 134
antiracist training, 160
anxiety, 75
arguments, cultural differences in dealing with, 116–119
Arnold, E., 134
arranged marriage, 104

assessment:
   and intervention, link between, 11–14
   of families, 7
assumptions:
   of common perspectives, in shared projects, dangers of, 150–152
   personal, examining, 45
asylum-seeking, 52, 67, 83
Atkar, S., 9
attachments, recursive influences of, 43
Avigad, J., 82–94
Azuma, H., 28

Baker, J., 4
Baldwin, N., 9
Banks, N., 114
Barn, R., 3–15, 69
Bartlett, C., 22
Bateson, G., 39, 103, 159
Batta, I., 7
Bebbington, A. C., 5
Bedward movement, 54
Berkow, D. N., 23
Berridge, D., 4, 12

INDEX

Black Star Line, 54
Bocher, S., 119
Bond, M. H., 28
Boorhem, H., 162
Box, L., 11, 12
Boyd-Franklin, N., 50, 73, 112, 122
Brock, G. W., 130
Burck, C., 97
Burke, A., 112
Burman, E., 100
Burns, L., 148–162
Butt, J., 11, 12
Byng-Hall, J., 88, 123

Cacas, J. M., 28
Caesar, G., 4
Callanan, P., 128
CAMHS, 69, 70, 71, 97
Carby, H., 5
Carter, B., 97, 114, 115, 123
case studies:
    child protection and parental
        authority (G family), 72, 76
    cross-cultural work in residential
        setting, 115–123
    culturally meaningful patterning,
        40–44
    culturally specific intervention to
        reconnect mother, 57–59
    cultural sameness and cultural
        difference, 102–103
    eco-map, 74
    mixed-cultural team, 64–67
    racial attitudes in health team, 61–62
    same–same therapy, 59–60
    worker's reaction to client's racist
        comments, 101–102
    working with refugees, 85–94
Cecchin, G., 37, 106, 107
Chand, A., 9
change, encouraging and reinforcing, 76–77
Cheetham, J., 4, 11
child and adolescent mental health
    service (CAMHS), 69, 70, 71, 97
child protection:
    discipline, issues of, 72, 121
    see also punishment
    register, 4, 8, 69, 72, 81
    system, 69–72
    feelings of parents towards, 75
    workers in, 77, 127
child-rearing methods, socially
    unacceptable, 72
children:
    care system:
        entry into, 5, 10–11
        overrepresentation of ethnic
            minorities in, 69–70
    discipline, cultural attitudes
        towards, 8, 120–121
    see also punishment
    and family, re-establishing,
        connections between, 74–75
    fostering of, 6, 10, 12, 13, 40
    as gatekeepers to new culture, 144
    inpatient psychiatric unit for, 85–94
    minority ethnic, proportion of, 8
    mixed-parentage, 11
    punishment of, *see* discipline;
        punishment
    sexualized behaviour of, 86, 116
        inappropriate, 27
    see also residential care
Children Act 1989, 10, 12, 72, 75
    Report, 14
child welfare, 3–15
Coleman, P., 70
collectivist culture:
    clients from, clinical practice with, 24–26
    and confidentiality, 31–32
    family function in, 24
    importance of values of, to ethnic-
        minority families, 31
    self in, 29
    society, 74
communicating, 83, 119
    blockage of, by assumptions and
        power inequalities, 145–146
    cross-culturally, 35–36
    in culturally sensible ways, 20
    ethnic-minority worker, 119, 128
    in families, 74
    in family therapy, 34–45
    fundamental need to, 34
    and interaction, patterns produced
        by, 44
    and prejudices, 37–38
    racial bonding as channel for, 115

INDEX

respect for parents, 72
and triggering of past experiences, effects of, 156
between workers, 83–94, 148–161
confidentiality, 31–32
connecting, 34, 62, 84, 103
  see also engaging; joining
Cooklin, A., 63, 144
"co-ordinated management of meaning", 154
Corey, G., 128
co-workers, disagreement/discomfort with, 152–156
Cronen, V., 154
Cross, W. E., Jr., 115
cross-cultural work (*passim*):
  barriers to, 27
  with colleagues, 148–162
  combatting oppressive practices, 122–124
  competence in, 26
  conflict of positions, 152
  eco-system approach to, 28–32
  emotional aspects of, 152, 157
  ethical, 44
  factors constraining, 99
  hazards, for professionals, 145–147
  ideas facilitating, 105–108
  lack of progress in, 96
  level of commitment in, 149
  level of engagement in, 160
  misperceptions in, 80
  and "not knowing", 44
  sameness and difference, 62–68
  taking risks in, 97–110, 111–130
  workshop on, 149
"cultural brokers", 122–123
cultural competence:
  of professionals, 26–27
  and therapeutic relationship, 26–27
cultural encapsulation, 127
cultural frames, different, navigating between, 96–97
cultural institutions, 39
"cultural lenses" (Hoffman), 38
culturally appropriate methods, seen by majority therapists as alien or pathological, 52
"cultural naiveté" (Dyche & Zayas), 79
cultural perspective, different, danger of explicating, 128

cultural practice, counselling and psychotherapy as forms of, 20
cultural sameness, as obstacle to creative thinking, 102
cultural shock, 119
culture, 10, 19–33
  continuity in, aspects of, 37–38
  definitions of, 20–21, 98
  of meaning, 39
  and disputes, differences in resolving, 116–119
  and ethnicity, 20–21
  fundamental similarities among, 101
  individualist vs. collectivist, 21–23
  making transitions between, 92
  as meaning system, 19–20
  new, psychological effects of moving to, 119
  prejudicial view of, 38, 44
  and the self, 23–24
  status of husband in, 145–146
  and transracial placements, 10
curiosity, 98, 107–109, 121
cycles of events, negative, 77

d'Ardenne, P., 115
daughters, attachment of to mother, 58
delusions and mistakes, culturally meaningful, 40
Department of Health, 14
depression, 40
development:
  personal, 32, 67, 100, 104, 129, 131–147, 148–162
  professional, 50, 67, 100, 104, 129, 131–147, 148–162
Dewey, J., 38
difference, 110
  divisiveness of, 150–152
dilemma(s):
  ethical, 123
  exploring, 123
  placement of children, 11
  in presenting different cultural perspective, 128
  as "racial other", 124
  of speaking one's mind, 149, 154, 158, 162
  in therapy, 98, 111–130
  work with refugee family, 83–94

discipline, cultural attitudes towards, 8, 120–121
  see also punishment
discrimination, 109, 119
  experiences of, 155–156
  institutional, 36
  unconscious and implicit aspects of, 37–38
discriminatory behaviour, in helping professions, 8–11
dispute resolution, verbal vs. physical, 119
Divine, D., 10
Douglas, M., 35
Down, G., 145
drug abuse, 30, 60, 64
Du Bois, W. E. B., 54
Dutt, R., 7, 9
Dyche, L., 79

each-to-their-own therapies:
  majority, 59–62
  minority, 51–59
"eco-map", 73–75
emotional commitment, 157
empathy, as a therapeutic tool, 53, 113, 117, 125
engaging:
  with different frames, 97
  with family, 71–73, 88
  see also connecting; joining
Epston, D., 76
ethics:
  issues, 34–46, 50
  professional code of, 119
ethnicity: *see* culture; race
ethnic monitoring, 14–15
ethnic minorities:
  percentage of total population, 3
  political sensitivity surrounding, 121
ethnic-minority worker(s):
  as ambassador for a culture, 113
  as best match for family, 127
  as "cultural expert", 113
  lack of, in field of therapy, 113
  in role of a white person, 124
  suspicion towards, 123
  see also therapist; worker
ethnocentric biases, 33

Eve, M., 140
extended family, 24, 29, 30, 32, 74, 104, 112, 116

family(ies) (*passsim*):
  cultural differences within, 105
  different race, arguments between, 116–119
  dislocated, 73
  extended, 24, 29, 30, 32, 74, 104, 112, 116
  group working, 12
  minority ethnic, pathologizing of, 5, 8
  placements:
    for minority ethnic children, 10–11
    for mixed-parentage children, 11
  status of husband in, 145–146
  and systemic approach, seen as part of larger systems, 112
  systems, impact of external struggles on, 52
  use of as a resource, 30
  values, loyalty to, 142–145
  work with, same-culture vs. cross-culture, 49–68
Family Rights Group, 10
Family Welfare Association, 5
Fatimilehin, I., 70
fear/distress/anger, communicating, 93
feedback, from client, 106
Ferdinand, D., 5
Fernando, S., 24, 27, 28, 30, 97
Fitzherbert, K., 5, 7
Flaskas, C., 108
Fordham, M., 43
foster care, 6, 12
  racial matching, 10
foster-carers, 10, 13, 40
  support for, 10–11, 14
Fruggeri, L., 105, 108
Furnham, A., 119

Garnett, L., 5
Garvey, M., 54
Geertz, C., 38
Gellner, E., 35
gender, 134

and social functioning in children, 138–140
generalizations and assumptions, trap of, 126
genogram, 74, 93
 and eco-maps, 74
 as team exercise, 63–64
Gibbons, J., 8, 9
Gill, O., 10, 13
good-enough relationship, establishing, 103
Goolishian, H., 44
Gorell Barnes, G., 122, 133–147
Gowrisunkur, J., 100
grandparents, 23, 29
grooming, as means for bonding, 58–59
guesswork, in therapy, 43

Haley, J., 30
Hall, C. C. I., 24, 27
Hall, E. T., 22
Harding, S., 134
Hardy, K., 146
Haste, H., 138
Hawkes, B., 58
health, "universal" definition of, 19
Helms, J. E., 114, 115
helplessness, feelings of, 127
Henriques, J., 37
hierarchies:
 among minority groups, 54
 rejection of, 156
Hildebrand, J., 100
Hinings, D., 13
Ho, D. Y. F., 23
Hoffman, L., 38
Holdstock, T. L., 23
Holland, S., 51
homophobia, 60
homosexuality, 51, 52, 54, 60
hooks, b., 156
host culture, 97, 121, 125
Howe, D., 13
Howitt, D., 23, 27, 28
Huang, L. N., 24
Humphries, C., 9
Hundleby, M., 5
husband, cultural status of, 145–146
Hylton, C., 25, 31

identity, 158
 inferior, process of dismantling, 51
 sense of self through relationships, 83–84
immigration laws, 6
Ince, L., 11, 13
indigenous therapies, 27–28
inferior identity, process of dismantling, 51
inferiority/superiority, belief in, in contemporary society, 61
"insider/outsider" experiences, 158–161
institutional racism, 5, 8, 9, 36–38, 45, 95–96
institutions:
 culture of, 98
 support for workers within, 98
interventions, 11–14
 approach to, of indigenous therapies, 27
 culturally diverse, 28
 discussing relevance of with families, 79
 strategies for, coordinating, 78
irreverence, 107

Jackson, B., 10, 13, 56
Jackson, G. G., 51, 56
Johnson, K., 154
Johnson, M., 8
joining, 45, 52
 see also connecting; engaging
Jones, A., 12
Jones, E., 108
Jung, C. G., 123

Kakar, S., 29
Kareem, J., 50, 51, 63, 97
Kay, J., 156
Kemps, C., 148–162
Khan, S., 95–110
Kitayama, S., 21, 23
Knappert, K., 20, 26
knowing, 103–105, 160
Kohut, H., 39
Kornreich, R., 8
Krause, I.-B., 34–46, 97

Lambert, L., 5, 10

182   INDEX

Landrine, H., 23, 24, 29
Lane, G., 37, 107
language:
   and assimilation, 144
   as barrier in therapy, 26–27
   creating meanings through, 96
   definition of ethnic group, 21
   as emphasizing difference, 101
   influences on, 154
   insider/outsider experiences, 158
   oppressive, 62
   shared, and racism, 36
   and transracial placements, 10
   work with refugee families, 83–87
Lannamann, J., 154
Laszloffy, T., 146
Lau, A., 50, 97
Lawrence, E., 5
Lawrence, Stephen, 36, 44
Leary, K., 26
Lee, C., 128
lesbians, 51, 54
Lesser, R. C., 23
Levine, R. V., 22
Lieberman, S., 63
linguistic skills, 21, 26
Lipsedge, M., 24
Littlewood, R., 24, 50, 51, 63, 97
Lloyd, B., 138
Lobatto, W., 69–81
Lomov, F. F., 20
loyalty, to family values, 142–145

Maccoby, E. E., 138
MacDonald, S., 69
MacKinnon, L., 75
Macpherson, Sir W., 36, 37, 38, 44
Macpherson Report, 36, 44, 45, 95
Mahtani, A., 115
Maitra, B., 25, 29
majority cultures, privileges of, 59
MAMA (East African Women's
   Group), 156
Markus, H. R., 21, 23
marriage, arranged, 104
Mason, B., 106, 123
Mazower, M., 141
Mbiti, J., 23
McCann, D., 145
McCulloch, J., 7
McGee, D. P., 51, 56

McGoldrick, M., 97
meaning, in culture, definition of, 39
mental illness, 41
Messent, P., 69–81
Miles, J. B., 5
Miller, A., 64, 97
Minnis, H., 14
minority ethnic communities:
   internalized negative views of, 53
   social position of, in relation to
     majority, 51
   transitions and changes in, 104
minority ethnic family(ies) (*passim*):
   and child abuse, 8
   discipline, cultural attitudes
     towards, 8, 120–121
   see also punishment
   immigration of, 4–5
   negative attitudes towards, 70, 71
   and parent–child conflict, 12
   values, lack of understanding of,
     69–70
minority ethnic therapist(s), 50, 52, 53,
   56, 61, 67
   lack of, in family therapy
     institutions, 99
   as role model, 53, 75
minority therapies, disseminating
   ideas about, 56
mixed-parentage children, 4, 11, 13
Modood, T., 6
Moghaddam, F., 24
Moncayo, R., 24
Montagu, A., 21
Moore, M. A., 27
Morris, H. S., 21
mother, bonding of child with, 58
multiculturalism, 3, 5, 6
Murrell, M., 70

National Children's Home, 4
negative cycles:
   of events, 77
   of interaction, 70, 77, 78, 80
Neihart, M., 130
Neimeyer, G. J., 27
networking, with other profesionals,
   87
"news of a difference" (Bateson), 103
Ney, S., 35
Niabingies movement, 54

Nichols, G., 156
Norford, L., 13
not connecting, seen as pathological, 84
"not knowing", 44, 103–105

O'Brian, C., 27, 64
Ochs, E., 139
openness, fear of, 127
oppression, 53, 119, 162
oppressive practices, combatting, 122
Owusu-Bempah, K., 19–33

Page, R. C., 23
Paniagua, F. A., 24
Parchment, M., 4
Paré, D., 98, 100
parents:
    authority of, within family, 72
    "safe", re-establishing, 75–76
    communicating respect for, 72
    good intentions of, communicating respect for, 71–73
    involvement of, in disputes between children, 118
    meeting with, without children, 72
    re-empowering, 75
    and statutory organizations, explaining about, 75
Parker, W. M., 27
past experiences, triggering of residues of, 156
patterning, 44
    and culture, 39–40
Peavy, R. V., 20
Pedersen, P., 122, 127
Penketh, L., 12
Perelberg, R. J., 97
Perlesz, A., 108
personal development, 32, 67, 100, 104, 129, 131–147, 148–162
Phillips, M., 7, 9
physical abuse, 8
polarization, avoiding, 80
political asylum, 116
Pooley, J., 82–94
Post-Adoption Centre, London, 13
power, 59
    abuse of, 45
    dynamic of, between therapist and client, 108
    hierarchy of, 49
    inequalities of, 151, 161
    issues of, 51
practitioners, cultural competence of, 26–27
prejudice(s):
    as condition for communicating, 37–38
    cybernetics of, 106
Prilleltensky, I., 123
privacy, 31
professional abilities, and race of therapist, 114
professional development, 50, 67, 100, 104, 129, 131–147, 148–162
professionalism, calling into question of, 117
provocation, instinctual reaction to, 119
public humiliation, 52
punishment, 8, 9, 72, 121
    attitudes towards, 8, 120–121
    and child-protection concerns, 72
    inappropriate, 76
    reaction to Western forms of, 120

Qureshi, T., 12

race:
    and child welfare, 3–15
    and culture, unwillingness to address, 95
    deconstruction of, 146
    and difference, issues of, 65
    issues of:
        addressing, at conferences, 50
        anxiety raised by, 26
        within team, 65, 66
        in training, 27
        unwillingness to address, 95–96, 99, 100
        for workers, 121–129
    -related issues, speaking out on, dilemmas arising from, 124
    relations, 36
    shared with client, 113–115
    synonymous with "culture" and "ethnicity", 21
    and transracial placements, 10
racial beliefs, vicious cycle of, 70

racial difference, addressing:
  with client families, 79–80
  with other agencies, 78–79
  between project members, 80–81
racial discrimination, 3, 9, 156
  "genetic", 155
racial group, cultural differences
    within, 99
racial harassment, 9
"racial other", 123
racial role, adopting opposite
    (exercise), 124
racism:
  accusation of, experiences of, 145
  and assessment, 7–10
  in client, 60
  covert foundations of, 144
  damaging impact of, 95
  deconstructing, 145
  experiences of, and professional
      development, 109, 141, 145–
      147
  institutional, 5, 8, 9, 36–38, 45, 95–
      96
  internalized, 143
  within minority groups, 53
  oppressive practices, perpetuation
      of, 112
  and shared ethnicity, 36
  systemic effect of, 49
  taboo against discussion of in
      family, 143
  within therapeutic profession, 50–
      53
racist comments, by patient, 59–61
racist discourse, internalized, as part
    of family values, 142–145
racist thinking, persistence of, 135
Rashid, H., 7
Rashid, S., 7, 13
Ray, W. A., 37, 107
referral, 86–87
reflecting conversations, 86–87, 89–91
refugee families, working with, 52, 83–
    94
"refugee identity", 84
religion, 10, 20, 64, 137, 139
  and transracial placements, 10
research studies:
  creative working, and dialogue
    about dilemmas, 123
minority ethnic families:
  in Britain, 31
  and care systems, 4–15
  working with, 56
race, as personal and political issue,
    114–115
residential care, 5, 10, 14, 120
residential unit, working in, 112–121
respect, 108
  for parents, communicating, 71–73
responsibility, individual and
    collective, 109–110
responsible practice, issues of, 128
Richards, A., 11
Richards, G., 111–131
Richeport-Haley, M., 19, 24, 30
risk-taking, 34, 95–110, 111–112, 123,
    124, 126, 130
Robinson, L., 14
Roland, A., 23, 29
Rossiter, A., 123
Rowe, J., 5, 10, 12, 13, 69
Rushton, A., 14

Safaris, M., 140
Said, E., 143
same-culture vs. cross-culture family
    therapy, 49–68
sameness, circularity of, 60
same–same therapy, 50, 113
  benefit of, 52
  conflicts of interests in, 126
  intercultural therapy within, 63
  support for minority staff, 55–59
  suspicion aroused by, 56
Sangha, K., 100
Sassoon, S., 82
Sawyerr, A., 129
Scarman, Lord, 36
Scarman Report, 36
Schneider-Corey, M., 128
school:
  behavioural problems at, 72
  difficulties at, 86
  involving in change, 76–77
  involving parents in, 79
  staff, and minority parents,
      negative cycles of interaction
      between, 78

self, 19–33
  -appraisal, 52
  in collectivist culture, 29
  cultural perceptions of, 23
  -esteem, boosting, 77
  -image, improving, 78
  -loathing, 53
  -referral, rarity of, 70
  -reflection, 108
    by therapist, 43, 46
  -reflexivity, 98, 108
  socially constructed aspects of, 134
  -validation, 51
  Western notion of, 23
sense of community, deep, 31
sexual abuse, 8, 9, 57, 102
sexualized behaviour, in children, 86, 116
shame, sense of, 52
Shiang, J., 23, 25
Silavwe, G. W., 31, 32
Simon, R. J., 13
Sinclair, R., 5, 14
Small, J., 7, 10
Smith, N., 7
Smith, P. B., 28
social constructionism, 96, 145
social majority, need for self-appraisal by, 51–53
social psychology, 37
social roles, 23
social workers, 8, 40, 41, 70–72, 80, 101, 113, 134, 135
  negative reactions to, 69
social-work policy and practice, 7–15
sociocultural processes, and working with clients, 108
Speed, B., 97
status quo, freedom to question, 157
statutory agencies:
  anxiety generated by contact with, 75
  explaining to parents, 72, 75
  wariness of families towards, 9
Steadman, C., 139
stealing, 88, 90, 91
stereotypes, 124
  cultural, 120
"strange loop", 154
Sue, D. W., 24, 26, 115, 126

Sue, S., 24
superiority, assumptions of,
  by clients, in relation to minorities, 51
  hierarchy of, 54
  as professionals, 45
  stereotypical, 53, 61
support networks, 7, 11, 25
support system, 31, 69, 84
  family/community, 25, 31
  psychologies, 34
Syal, M., 156
systemic approach, and racism, 112

Taylor, C., 139
teacher(s), 76–79, 99, 118
  discussing racism with, 78–79
team:
  credibility of, 77
  cross-cultural, 71–81
  divisions among, 89
  extreme feelings endured by, 93
  multicultural, 123
  resistance to change in, 63–64
  training, need for, 64
theft, 88, 90, 91
therapeutic relationship:
  and cultural difference, 97
  difficulties in establishing, 84
  as encounter between two cultures, 100, 109–110
  interventions:
    and assessment, link between, 11–14
    culturally diverse, 28
    discussing relevance of with families, 79
    and indigenous therapies, 27–28
    social model for, espoused by minorities, 51
    strategies for, coordinating, 78
  processes impacting on, 108
  sociocultural dimensions affecting, 109
therapist(s):
  and client:
    differences and similarities between, 101–103
    dynamic of power between, 108
  culture of, as factor in therapy, 100

therapist(s) *(continued)*:
  family backgrounds/experiences of, 63
  minority ethnic, 101
  safe-enough environment for, 123
  vulnerabilities of, revealing and sharing with colleagues, 157
  white, understanding of systemic effect of racism, 49–51
  see also workers
therapy *(passim)*:
  cross-ethnic, 19–33
  drop out from, 23
  "each to their own", 49–62
  ethics in, 34–46
  goals of, making explicit, 73
  guesswork, 43
  indigenous, 27–28
  intercultural, 100
  psychodynamic, 116
  same-culture vs. cross-culture, 49–68
  uncertainty in, 34–46
  white, value base of, 50
  see also same–same therapy
Thoburn, J., 13
Thomas, L. K., 7, 49–68, 52, 53, 64, 67, 114, 146
time, cultural perspectives of, 22
tokenism, 154
training:
  developing ego strength to express cultural knowledge, 128
  lack of focus in on emotional aspects, 152
  limits of, 104–105
  institutions, 98, 99, 100
    gender as visible difference in, 99
    promoting cross-cultural work in, 109
trauma, extreme, 86
Triandis, H. C., 21, 22

uncertainty, 36–38, 44
  therapist's attempts to manage, 43
understanding, "experience-near" or "experience-far" (Geertz), 38

violence, 128
  cultural contexts of, 120–121

voices, dominant and marginalized, 144

Wakefield, J. C., 28, 29
Walker, A., 156
Walsh-Bowers, R., 123
Watts-Jones, D., 74
Wenman, H., 12, 21
Western cultures, individualist, 22, 31
Western framework, for therapy, 24–27, 31–33, 45, 50, 87, 92, 118
  and assessment, 7
  psychoanalytic, 43
Western orthodox therapies, loss of credibility as value-free, 51
Western standards, professional code of ethics, 119
White, M., 76
white identity, lack of discussion about, 122
whiteness, 122
  identity issues around, 59
white supremacy, 61
Whyte, S. R., 38
Wijsen, F., 19
witchcraft, 41–42
Wittgenstein, L., 35
women, oppressive environments for, 104
worker(s):
  appointed because of race, 114
  cultural competence of, 26–27
  dichotomies faced by, 119
  ethnic, higher expectations from, 114
  experiences of accusation of racism, 145–146
  neutral (from third culture), 117
  support for and between, 55–59, 61–62, 80
  white, in role of ethnic-minority person, 124
  see also therapist
World Health Organization, 19

Young, L., 156

Zayas, L., 79
Zephaniah, B., 156
Zygmond, M. J., 162

Printed in Great Britain
by Amazon